THE INC
(INDIAN NATIONAL CONGRESS)

A PARTY OF IDEA AND CHANGES

SK NIGAM

ISBN 979-8-89186-423-8

Contents

Preface

24, Akbar Road, New Delhi, January 24, 2019 While sipping hot tea in the canteen of the Congress Party office in the bone-chilling cold, the political heat has increased in the AICC campus with our Eastern Uttar Pradesh, which seems to becoming crucial to the great political war of 2019 once again in the entire country. The reason for Priyanka Gandhi Vadra getting an official role in Congress and being made in-charge of Eastern Uttar Pradesh. In such a situation, the 42 major constituencies falling under his charge also include Prime Minister Modi's seat Varanasi and Gorakhpur, the stronghold of the state Chief Minister. Lok Sabha elections are coming closer, everyone's eyes are on ticket distribution and the desire to get the ticket is increasing the restlessness among the Congress leaders, including a newbie like me. Now all the Congress leaders of Purvanchal have started feeling that if they can meet Mrs. Priyanka Gandhi Vadra then it may be easier to get the ticket. In such a situation, I also tried to meet her four times at her residence 35, Lodhi Estate, New Delhi, where even after all the checking and a long wait, the SPG did not allow pedestrian party workers like me to meet her due to security reasons. Some people coming in big and expensive vehicles continued to get entry. After repeated requests, on Feb 4, 2019 a generous SPG personnel suggested me to access the office of Rajiv Gandhi Foundation, where I could easily meet Priyanka ji. Without wasting any time, hired an auto and soon I was standing in front of the steps of Rajiv Gandhi Foundation, Jawahar Bhawan, Rajendra Prasad Road. It was told at the office reception that to meet Ma'am, permission would have to be taken from Mr. Dheeraj Srivastava and to meet Mr. Srivastava, an appointment would have to be taken from Mr. Yogendra. Which was nothing more than procrastination.

Feb 6, 2019, she took over the charge after her husband Mr. Robert Vadra left the ED office amid slogans like "Desh ki Aandhi Priyanka Gandhi". After this she met party workers that is why most of the tussle is being seen inside the Congress office campus. Although it was not possible for me to meet her due to the huge push and pull of the enthusiastic workers, but for the first time, I got the opportunity to see in person that courageous, patient and dutiful woman, whom till date I had been able to see only on television, newspapers and magazines. The whole of February and March was spent in following her Lucknow road show and meetings at UPCC Feb, 11 to 14, climbing the stairs of Rajiv Gandhi Foundation and unsuccessfully trying to contact both Mr. Dheeraj and Mr. Yogendra through mobile and message. And after trying hard to get the ticket, I could not even meet Mrs. Priyanka Gandhi Vadra. The party declared ex MP Rajesh Mishra imported from Varanasi as its candidate from Salempur Lok Sabha constituency. However, I was offered the Ballia seat of the Congress alliance by Babu Singh Kushwaha's Jan Adhikar Party, which was given to a local leader Amarjeet Chaudhary after my refusal and advice. Which proved to be the biggest political mistake of my life. As the party started distributing tickets for the Lok Sabha Elections 2019, news of displeasure of the disappointed candidates also kept making headlines. In fact, the formula for distribution of tickets is such that it creates resentment among those who get tickets and resentment over seats among those who are deprived of them.

The idea of writing this book stems from experience that is very personal to me. Thus, I agree that complete neutrality is not possible, but it is okay to approach it logically as far as possible. Uttar Pradesh with the largest number of seats in the Parliament – the Gateway of Parliament ; The state which was used to be the axis of Congress and its national politics ever, but today the situation is so pity that the representation of party has reached the minimum level in the state. I meet to the voters and grass root workers of the old Congress ideology and came to know that they still have pride in the party and in the freedom and progress of the country, on their old leaders, who despite being out of power for more than three decades fighting the political battle of the Congress with great devotion. Those who are crushed by the present regime and who sometimes do not have the courage to hope that their days will turn, but who still have hope and who have faith in their heart.

Today, when a nationwide exercise is going on to save democracy. Forced to have no political or dynastical support, a democracy activist is useless at this time when an autocratic power strangling the country's democracy. Sometimes get bored of this idleness and with my political non-existence then I try to look at this, the way one looks at a natural disaster like flood. I look back my childhood days, when people in my neighbourhood asked me to imitate our favourite Prime Minister, late Rajiv Gandhi, I would immediately make a shawl out of any cloth in his style and start walking around. What vague images had produced in my mind at that time, and what changes had been made in them by the new experience, but it is always present. It kept changing with the times and present day reality combined to make it a strange mix. It made me strong as well as weakened, because of what had happened around me – the death of my father in my teens, the struggle for bread, the condition of poverty and resourceful people.

As I grew up and got involved in works that could generate the necessary resources, used to get lost in the daydream of becoming a Congress MP during my research to be familiar with the Indian political scenario and electoral process which overrun it as described in my book Electoral Jugaad. But this was not enough to satisfy the questions that were arising in my mind. If we leave aside the narrow mindset of some of its regional leaders, then what is Congress Party after all? What were its objectives in the past; What was the thing that gave it strength? How has it lost its old vigour? What is its proper place in the political environment of India in future? But the future comes later, first we have the present, and behind this present there is a long and complicated past, which shaped the present, therefore, it is necessary to understand things Since I have resorted to the past.

Working in a small wing of UPCC (NGO Cell, which is worthless as told by Mr. Sachin Naik, Secretary AICC at Salempur 2019 LS Candidate's interview) of its vast organization, I deciphered the history of congress. I was deeply impressed by the power of thought, the political language of its leaders specially Pandit Jawahar Lal Nehru that was behind this party. Now that the memories of the Congress fight for the country's independence are fading and the new generation specially millennials, who are being misled by modern communication technology with deep fake electoral strategies, my reaction to the Congress party may be seem sentimental to it.

However Like other political parties, I do not imagine the Congress party too idealistically, and as far as possible, I avoid thinking of it even in my dreams. I would like to think of it not as an old political party, but as a nurturer of independent ideas. It may be that since I do not expect anything from it, I am not disappointed. I found it more than expected due to my inclination towards centre left socialism. The Congress and the reasons for its decline or fall is an interesting search. Nevertheless, the reasons for this decline are quite obvious. How it fell behind in the race of technology, and BJP, which was backward in many aspects from the beginning, with the rise of Modi, became the leader in the company of technological progress, behind which data science and social media were the strength. By use of new technology BJP 's political power increased a lot and it became possible for them to spread in Uttar Pradesh and occupy maximum Lok Sabha and Vidhan Sabha seats and this is the story not only of Uttar Pradesh but also of maximum states of the country.

How this happened, it is a bit difficult to tell, because the Congressmen were not backward in the skills of politics in the olden days. As the decades go by, we see the decline of this skill. political will decreases, creative power vanishes and in its place imitation and deceit comes. Where revolutionary ideas had tried to show the way to the whole country, now the rhetorical commentators bring their political hypocrisy. The spirit and morality of national development, which we find equal in the olden times, and due to which the country could have progressed even more, turns into political drunkenness, luxury and corruption. The edge of Congress slows down, carrying the political burden of decades as if people live in the past. The heavy weight of the past crushes it in General

Elections 2014 and a kind of unconsciousness comes over it. It is not surprising that the Congress came in such a state of fatigue in 2019 General Elections. Thus it remained where it was, while some other political parties of India moved forward.

To fight for the revival of the Congress and to rekindle its political vitality, this book will be able to create enthusiasm among the Indian citizens of the new century, especially the youth, for the Party. Since this objective is in front of me and some regional leaders of Congress keep on wondering at my stubbornness and stupid methods. Whether I did stupidity or not, it will be known only later. I have set my aims high and my eyes have been fixed on things far away. If seen from the point of view of current political scenario, I may have often done stupid things, but I have not let my main objective disappear from my eyes and this objective of mine is to awaken the entire Congress leadership, their consciousness and soul. And definitely they have to warn about their political laxity and the state of thoughtlessness. The present condition of the people in our country is like a strange mess of things, extreme poverty and unemployment, increasing capitalist dominance in politics and biased attitude of national media and somewhat superficial modernity of a misinformed larger section of the middle class. In fact, the aim of this book is to create political awareness in them – knowing that other things will follow automatically.

Recently two major events the Bharat Jodo Yatra and Presidential Election of the party have brought significant change within and outside Congress recently. This change has endured the party to emphasize its internal democracy and its commitment to an inclusive and right-based politics. Though, there is a daunting to rejuvenate the party, but nevertheless, it isn't impossible. Undoubtedly, under duo leadership of Rahul Gandhi and Mallikarjun Kharge, there is substantial hope of the rejuvenation of the party. The resounding victory in the Himachal Pradesh Assembly Elections 2022, Karnataka and Telangana Assembly Elections 2023 and getting greater number of votes than BJP in Rajasthan, Madhya Pradesh and Chhattisgarh could be seen as a new beginning.

Ultimately a living citizen should be one who can face the socio-political issues of today. Therefore, in order to fulfil my civic duty, I have now put aside my sense of political insignificance and taken up the pen so that I can create awareness about our democracy and the Indian National Congress. Heartfelt thanks to you for supporting me in this endeavour.

– **Savya Sachi Krishnan Nigam**

Indian National Congress and the Role in Indian Independence: A Brief History

The exploitation and brutality doesn't last for much, so did, the mutiny which was against the tyrannical suppression and exploitation of Indians, finally brought the East India Company almost on its knees. Thou, the beginning of revolt was from the barracks in Meerut, subsequently spread wide and across at least in the Northern India; making unification among all forces such as the peasant of Awadh, Sepoys from the barracks of Bengal to Meerut, the Queen of Jhansi, and the last Mughal emperor, Bahadur Shah Zafar had subverted into the technical advanced British cavalry and infantry, indeed almost shaken the roots of the trading company, who ventured for the possible rule in India. But as it is a saying that in a love and war no one can predict till the curtain is drawn, so did it happen here too, the consequences couldn't be judged. Things changed dramatically, the thunderstorm of 1857 mutiny met its end in 1859, ultimately with seizure of Delhi by the Britishers, and the trajectory of the last Mughal Empire, Bahadur Shah Zafar. Eventually the high hopes of India's freedom and the last nail into the British coffin was tarnished. And thereafter India witnessed a long silence.

However, it wasn't just defeat of Indians, but the 1857 revolt was also the eye opener for Britishers too. The revolt succeeded in conveying a message that Indians were now passionate about their 'Azaadi' (freedom), and therefore wouldn't let the British forces rob and suppress them anymore. Thus, the British Government brought several drastic changes in their policies to rule in India. Among them the most significant was the end of the 'East India Company' hegemony, and beginning of direct British rule under the British Crown.

In England almost all sections of the political opinion opined that East India Company's economic and administrative policies were responsible for the outbreak of the rebellion. Therefore, the British Crown brought several major changes as well as blow to some of the repressive policies of the East India Company, among them was the Doctrine of Lapse, also they initiated some lucrative policies to appease the Indian, among them was the commencement of the institute for Indian Civil Service Examination and inclusion of the Indians was the major implementation to attract the educated Indian youth.

Nevertheless, it is an open secret that behind the so-called liberal face of the whites, the reality was haunting and humiliating the Indian masses. In fact, thousands and thousands Indian were sleuthed by the Britishers, though no one has exact data but certainly, the figure is beyond imagination. In an interview to the Guardian, Misra, the author of the book, 'War of Civilization: AD 1857 stated, "It was a holocaust, where one million disappeared. It was a necessary holocaust from the British point of view because they thought the only way to win was to destroy entire populations in towns and villages. It was simple and brutal. Indians who stood in their way were killed. But its scale has been kept secret." How far is that argument correct, but certainly numerous Indians were massacred in carnage.

Whatever be, one thing was certain that the people's early optimistic approach later transferred into disappointment. And the next two decades after the failed mutiny were the years of almost silence, but it won't be correct to jump to the conclusion that people were forgotten the pain and anguish for the martyrs who were brutally massacred by Britishers. Perhaps, sung and unsung heroes of the mutiny were the part of their long-lasting memories; their stories of sacrifice, courage and bravery was talked, sung and narrated as a heroic tales at the Chaupals (a pavement) of villages and at the corners and squares of towns in the country. However, it is also true that there wasn't any commotion in the society for yet another rebel, and that is why it has been observed that the period saw the emergence of reformist organizations and elite leaders for the next few decades. Meanwhile, the British Raj continued its expansion policy, but cautiously and great care, whereas, on the other hand, the Indian (especially elites) used the situation to bargain with British rule for their own interests. Certainly, most of the organizations of the time were dominated by wealthy and aristocratic elements. These organizations wanted to achieve administrative reforms, associations of Indians with administration, and expansion of education were the main quest of the time.

Awakening Call – The establishment of the National Congress (INC) in December 1885. This was by no means an accidental event, but was the hype of political awakening and anxiety among the wealthy and elite Indians, who played a pivotal role in forming the prominent political association with common objectives of their own well-being and serving as a bridge between the Government and the people. Besides, there were some other associations also established and worked to install the feeling of Nationalism in the people. Earlier the association like 'The Indian Association of Calcutta' discontented itself from pro-landlord and conservative policies of the British India Association and aimed to unify Indian people on a common political program. Definitely, many more such associations and individuals paved the path for modern Nationalism, in the form of Indian National Congress (INC).

No doubt, such handful organizations contributed significantly in arousing the political will and demands of the Indian public, but their area and activities were limited only into patches. nevertheless, these associations also devoid themselves from the political questions, and limited themselves to local issues. In the meanwhile, dissatisfaction in between the British and Indian intensified in the years between 1870s and 1880s because Arms Act (1878), Vernacular Press Act and later the introduction of Ilbert Bill added fuel to the fire which resultant in the furore of the Indians.

Thus, the enrage among Indian against the oppressive and racial attitude of the British in India, finally brought the educated Indians on their toe to think about some kind unity and to form an all-India organization. With the view point of an all-India political structure, several small organizations finally merged and culminated into a pan-India organization, i.e., the Indian National Congress, which later in the years not only resulted in spreading consciousness, but also awakened the zeal of Nationalism in the heart and minds of the Indians.

Impact of British Rule on the India

<table>
<tr><td valign="top">

Political

+ British Policy of conquest & expansion.
+ Revolt of 1857
+ Political & Administrative Unification for e.g., Rule of Law.

</td><td valign="top">

Socio-Cultural

+ Impact of Socio-Religious Movements
+ Spread of Modern & Western education
+ Role of Press & policy of racial discrimination.

</td><td valign="top">

Economic

+ Economic exploitation by British under different policies.
+ Economic policies with direct impact led to eco-Unification of the country.
+ Introduction of Railways

</td></tr>
</table>

The Early Years of Indian National Congress – Finally, in December 1885, the Indian National Congress established as a prominent political force and a pan-India political party with seventy-two delegates. These delegates were from all over the country, who met together at Bombay to formally give the structure to the party. The same party in the later years became the main force that led the liberation movement against the British hegemony. The prominent delegates who were the part of the newly formed Congress included Dadabhai Naorji, Surendranath Banerjee, Badruddin Tyabji, Pherozeshah Mehta, W. C. Banerjee, S. Subramania Iyer and Romesh Chander Dutt. The founding members also included an Englishman named Allan Octavian Hume, a former British servant. Womesh Chander Banerjee was elected president and Hume, himself, became the general secretary of the newly formed Indian National Congress. Ironically, Congress' formation to early-stage growth was under the shadow of undisputed British dominance or hegemony; i.e., under the patronage of British authorities and the rising class of Indians and Anglo-Indians educated in English language.

The congress beginning was humble, and nearly in the first twenty years (1885-1905), its function was primarily around debates and discussion about the British policy and its impact on India. Other than that, though reluctantly, but congress also surfaced some demands through resolutions that included civil rights administrative, constitutional and regarding economic policies which congress claimed were responsible for draining India's wealth because of unfair trade and the use of Indian taxes to pay high salaries to the British civil servants in India.

Despite the humble start, Congress able to garner some honour for itself by firmly taking stand on some of the issues, like emphasizing on the appointment of Indians in the government services and also demanded to open agricultural banks for the relief of peasantry. But all these were limited to plead and request.

Indeed, the newly formed Indian National Congress was the result of the emerging new middle class on the horizon of India, though they were still only countable but were spread across the country. This class was encouraged and jubilant because of education and of employment in the Indian civil services. This class raised the voice of protest against the discriminatory laws enacted by the British Government. Another issue that was raised by the Congress of than, was to increase the power of legislative councils; i.e., to include elected Indian representatives. The raised demand was fulfilled by the British government. In the economic sphere, the congress demanded for the introduction of modern industry and abolition of salt tax and so on.

However, despite some influential steps, nevertheless, Congress remained a reformist party, much relied on the guidance and praises of Britishers rather than their own efforts or attempt to address the issues of the ordinary people such poverty, lack of health care, social oppression and economic exploitation in the hands of the Britishers and local Zamindars in the rural India. Thus, Congress in the initial stage was the party of the elite class of Indian society who had very little to do with the ordinary people of India.

Back home, the ambience wasn't totally under the control of the congress, as Hindu viewed them supportive of Western culture, while Muslims saw it with suspicion as the party had significance domination of Hindus. These factors widened the gap, and thus became the victim of anger of both.

Nevertheless, despite the lucrative position of the Congressmen toward the British government, one cannot outwardly reject the importance of Congress. Perhaps, it can be said that in the first twenty years after the formation of Congress, the leaders successfully able to pursue and pressurized the British government for some changes and secondly able to advance the consciousness among the people of the pan-India to stand unitedly against the Britishers and their exploitative policies with the nationalistic approach; that later in years became the mile stone in the struggle against the Britishers.

The early years of the congress can be described as an of mixed colours. It was the period when Congress was relied upon petitions and prayers for immediate redress of urgent grievances in administration, but somewhat also motivated with certain degree of idealism in regard to India's political aspiration. Indeed, the leaders of the early years were later declared as the 'Moderates'. The Moderates or early Indian

Nationalists had faith in British liberalism, and therefore believed in peaceful co-existence and "politics of prayers".

Aim and objectives of the Indian National Congress – Despite the early politic of prayers, Congress always remain clear with its goal, therefore its ideology was based on the national unity, social inclusion and self-reliance. The party from the very beginning aimed and urged for a strong and united India would be necessary to withstand British rule and achieve independence. In the presidential address of the first session of the newly form Indian National Congress which was held in Mumbai in 1885, the main objectives of the party that were declared as follows-

- To promote and consolidate the feeling of National unity and to rid India of British colonial rule.
- To work for the cause of uplifting the lower classes and promoting education.
- To fight for the rights of women and minority communities.
- To protect and promote and promote India's cultural and heritage.
- Formulating popular demands and presenting them before the government.
- To promote healthy and friendly relations between nationalist and political workers from different parts of the country.
- To train and organize the public opinion in the country.

The two Poles within Congress – "Freedom is my birth right and I shall have it!" The late 19th and early years of 20th century witnessed the lounging of Bipin Chandra Pal, Bal Gangadhar Tilak and Lala Lajpat Rai from three corner of Indian soil i.e., from East, West and North on the board of the Indian nationalistic movement. They were critical to moderates and their "politics of prayers", and urged the people have believe on the importance of self-reliance and constructive work, and not on the 'good' intention of the government. They called for the swaraj. Later in 1905 the partition of Bengal infuriated the people of every corner of India. The moderates and radical jointly opposed the British act of malignity to curtail the influence of Bengali politicians, though both were the saviour of different ideas and approaches. In the meantime, the aggression of congress leaders stimulated the Britishers to become more hostile toward nationalists, in fact they branded nationalist as 'Disloyal', 'Seditious Brahmins' and "violent villain".

The call of radicals for the widespread protest against the partition of Bengal created rift between the moderates and radicals within congress. As the radical advocated mass mobilization and boycott of British institutions and goods, even some individual also suggested for the "revolutionary violence" to shake the British rule, whereas the moderates who dominated congress objected to such suggestion of the radicals, as they weren't ready for any sought of confrontation with British empire, nor was willing to spread the Swadeshi movement outside Bengal nor was ready to go beyond the boycott of foreign goods. Finally, the patience was getting thinner, and as a result in 1907, the two groups of congress split away. Thereafter, moderates dominated the congress, while the radical they continued work for the cause from outside. Later in 1915, both the groups once again came together.

The INC (A Party of Idea and Changes)

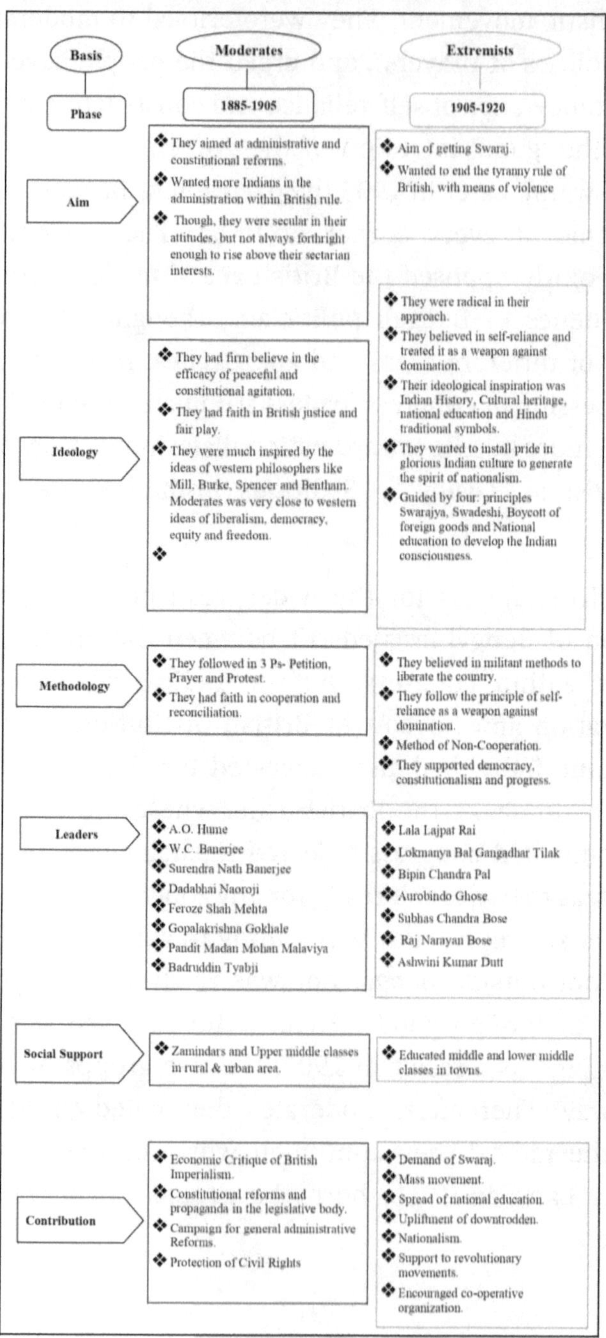

Basis	Moderates	Extremists
Phase	1885-1905	1905-1920
Aim	❖ They aimed at administrative and constitutional reforms. ❖ Wanted more Indians in the administration within British rule. ❖ Though, they were secular in their attitudes, but not always forthright enough to rise above their sectarian interests.	❖ Aim of getting Swaraj. ❖ Wanted to end the tyranny rule of British, with means of violence
Ideology	❖ They had firm believe in the efficacy of peaceful and constitutional agitation. ❖ They had faith in British justice and fair play. ❖ They were much inspired by the ideas of western philosophers like Mill, Burke, Spencer and Bentham. Moderates was very close to western ideas of liberalism, democracy, equity and freedom. ❖	❖ They were radical in their approach. ❖ They believed in self-reliance and treated it as a weapon against domination. ❖ Their ideological inspiration was Indian History, Cultural heritage, national education and Hindu traditional symbols. ❖ They wanted to install pride in glorious Indian culture to generate the spirit of nationalism. ❖ Guided by four: principles Swarajya, Swadeshi, Boycott of foreign goods and National education to develop the Indian consciousness.
Methodology	❖ They followed in 3 Ps- Petition, Prayer and Protest. ❖ They had faith in cooperation and reconciliation.	❖ They believed in militant methods to liberate the country. ❖ They follow the principle of self-reliance as a weapon against domination. ❖ Method of Non-Cooperation. ❖ They supported democracy, constitutionalism and progress.
Leaders	❖ A.O. Hume ❖ W.C. Banerjee ❖ Surendra Nath Banerjee ❖ Dadabhai Naoroji ❖ Feroze Shah Mehta ❖ Gopalakrishna Gokhale ❖ Pandit Madan Mohan Malaviya ❖ Badruddin Tyabji	❖ Lala Lajpat Rai ❖ Lokmanya Bal Gangadhar Tilak ❖ Bipin Chandra Pal ❖ Aurobindo Ghose ❖ Subhas Chandra Bose ❖ Raj Narayan Bose ❖ Ashwini Kumar Dutt
Social Support	❖ Zamindars and Upper middle classes in rural & urban area.	❖ Educated middle and lower middle classes in towns.
Contribution	❖ Economic Critique of British Imperialism. ❖ Constitutional reforms and propaganda in the legislative body. ❖ Campaign for general administrative Reforms. ❖ Protection of Civil Rights	❖ Demand of Swaraj. ❖ Mass movement. ❖ Spread of national education. ❖ Upliftment of downtrodden. ❖ Nationalism. ❖ Support to revolutionary movements. ❖ Encouraged co-operative organization.

Gandhi's appearance in the Indian National Movement – Mahatma Gandhi had evolved himself in a strong fight against racism, through a technique of passive resistance in South Africa in between 1894 and 1914, and thereafter returned to India in 1915. For the next few years, he toured various places in India to understand the people, and their needs as well as the overall situation of the country. Two years later, he started his political journey from Champaran, a district in Bihar where the peasants were plighted by their miserable and wanted to fight against the oppressive system of indigo plantation and the planters. It was the Gandhiji who took the initiative and succeeded in readdressing the grievances of the peasantry community with the support of prominent leaders like Rajendra Prasad and others.

Like many other colonies, the growth of modern nationalism was connected to the anti-colonial movement. Certainly, Indians began to discover their unity in the struggle with colonialism. However, the feeling of colonialism among the different groups and class varied, and therefore, their notions of freedom were not always the same. The circumstances made the moderates and radicals to come closer to each other, though the honeymoon between was for short span only, and ultimately it was Gandhi's effort who tried to forge the different groups together within one umbrella organisation Congress once again. However, this unity didn't emerge without conflicts in thoughts and ideas. The advent of Gandhi soon harvested a series of movements, some were bloomed from the womb of economic, while other were centric toward the socio-political cause.

The peasant movement of Champaran, Khadi, and textile workers movement of Ahmedabad in Gujrat were some of the exemplary movements of led by Gandhi and congress was the struggled for the economic cause, as the British polices brought the ruins to them. Whereas, the non-cooperation, Civil-Disobedience Movement, and the movement against Khilaft, which Gandhi saw as an opportunity to bring Muslims in a broader umbrella organization of a unified national movement. These movements were to promote socio-political awareness and unification among the Indian society for the mass mobilization and preparation for the mass struggle to bring British to their knees.

The Gandhi's arrival on the landscape of India, definitely consolidate the congress, as a political wing that inspired the leaders from all groups for liberation of India and further enhanced the movement to flourish against the British in a more organized form and determined with political motivation. However, at several occasions, the conflict of thoughts between leaders of radical and moderate groups continued to be an obstacle in the rise of the congress. But these conflicts came out with more political and organizational growth of congress as well as for overall Indian national movement.

The era of movement and inner conflict within congress – The Indian National Congress, which was established in 1885, has broadly developed over a time and through three stages of leadership. This leadership is often described as moderate, radical, or extremist and Gandhian philosophy, and this development was more or less concurrent with the three distinct phases, i.e., from 1885-1905, an era of moderate dominance; 1905-1919, a period of rift between the moderates and radicals; and the last phase was in between 1920-1947, which demonstrated the dominance of Gandhi's ideology in the Congress.

Despite the conflict and split in the leadership of Congress, the role of the Indian National Congress in the national movement cannot be ruled out. In fact, the Congress, under the direct or indirect guidance of Mahatma Gandhi, marked the first half of the 20th century as an era of long-lasting movement against the British. Though, there had been a mixed response from the people regarding Gandhi's non-violence, some movements leaped forward on the principal line of Gandhi's idea, but other times the people initiated the movement in their own methodologies. But they learned to fight against the whites and their suppressive rule. Let's have glimpses of the major movements that were led by Gandhi and Congress on the issue of conflict-

- **Satyagraha against Rowlatt Act** – In 1919, Gandhiji called for a satyagraha against the Rowlatt Act passed by the British. This was an act to curb fundamental rights such as freedom of expression and strengthen police powers. Mahatma and other congressmen criticised the Act as "devilish" and tyrannical. This movement turned out to be the first all-India struggle against the British, although largely restricted to cities. The movement against the Act saw unprecedented demonstrations and hartals in the country. To curb it, the British used brutal measures and massacres of the people; the testimony of the brutality is still in the memories of Indians in the form of the Jallianwala massacre, where the British officers ordered to shoot at the innocent people who had arrived there to celebrate Baisakhi. However, the country witnessed greater Hindu and Muslim unity.

- **Khilaft agitation and the Non-Cooperation Movement –** The First World War ended with the defeat of the Ottoman Empire, and thereby, the hostile British imposed several harsh treaties on the spiritual head of the Islamic world, i.e., the Khalifa. The Muslims of India formed the committee to defend the temporal power of the Khalifa. Gandhi saw the anguish among Muslims against Khilaft as an opportunity to bring Muslims under the umbrella of a unified national movement. Therefore, he convinced the congressmen as well as the leaders of the Khilaft Committee. This unification ultimately opened the doors for the non-cooperation against the British by surrendering the titles, boycotting of civil services, army, police, legislative councils, schools, and foreign goods. The non-cooperation movement, however, also intensified the tussle within the congress, especially on the issue of boycotting the legislative council. Finally, some seeking to comprise took place in the Nagpur session of Congress. Nevertheless, this movement led to a drastic decline in foreign goods between 1920 and 1922. But all this was only the tip of the iceberg.

- **Simon Commission Go Back –** In the backdrop of Simmon's arrival in India, the world economic condition was deepening from bad to worse because of the worldwide economic depression. Agricultural prices have been hard hit since 1926, and eventually collapsed after 1930. As a result, rural India was in tumult. Against this background, the new Tory government in Britain constituted a Statutory Commission, Sir John Simon was there to examine the workings of the constitutional system in India and suggest changes. But this commission didn't have a single

Indian member. Thus, at the time of the arrival of Simon to India, all parties, including the Congress and Muslim League, welcomed him with the slogan "Go back, Simon." In an effort to win over them, Viceroy Irwin, announced a vague offer of 'dominion status'. On the issue, the congress once again looked to be divided. The radicals like Subhash Chandra Bose and Jawahar Lal Nehru became more assertive, while the moderates, who were ready to work within the framework of British dominion, gradually lost their influence in congress. Finally, at the Lahore session congress, the demand for "Purn Swaraj" (full Independence) was formalised.

- **Dandi March and the Civil Disobedience Movement –** Mahatma Gandhi found that salt could be a powerful symbol that could unite the nation. Therefore, he demanded the abolishment of the salt tax as salt was something that was consumed by the rich and poor alike as an essential item. But contrary to demand, Irwin wasn't ready for negotiation, so Gandhiji started the famous salt march, accompanied by seventy-eight trustworthy volunteers, from the ashram of Sabarmati to the Gujrat coastal town of Dandi for over 240 miles. Thousands of men, women, and children gathered to listen to Gandhiji, while he was on the way to Dandi. This movement could be marked as the beginning of the civil-disobedience movement. Inspired by Gandhi, thousands and thousands of people around the country broke the salt law and manufactured salt. As the movement spread, a large-scale boycott of foreign clothes and picketing of liquor shops became part of the movement. In the villages too, the heat of the protest was felt in the form of violations of forest laws and resignations by the officials. Seeing the wide-scale demonstration, the colonial government began arresting the congress. The leaders, like Abdull Gafar Khan, a staunch Gandhi's disciple, were arrested, and later Mahatma Gandhi was taken into custody. In retaliation, the angry mob attacked the British government officials and the structure that represented the British symbol. Gandhi, finally, called off the movement and entered into a pact with Irwin on March 5, 1931, the very month when the revolutionary Bhagat Singh, Sukh Dev, and Raj Guru were executed by the Britishers.

- **Provincial Autonomy** – The people's struggle finally able to garner the much-awaited fruits when the Government of India Act – 1935, finally made its approval of provincial autonomy, and thereby, declared elections to the provincial legislatures in 1937. In the election, congress stunned everyone with its spectacular performance by bagging eight out of eleven provinces.

The years between 1917 to 1930s were the period of ups and downs for Congress politics and the Indian National Movement. The split within congress and then unification remained the landmark of congress. It was also the time when Gandhian magic played a pivotal role in a thriving series of anti-British movements. In fact, the spread of the national movement with the thought of nationalism developed a sense of collective belonging in the rural and urban areas of India. The period also witnessed different schools of thought in politics, and thereby, Congress also underwent challenges in politics as well as in the social arena. The mid-1920s witnessed the heat of two very different ideological organizations in the form of Rashtriya Swayamsevak Sangh and the Communist

Party on the outlet of the Indian political scenario; the former represented extreme right-wing politics and later believed in the ideology of the proletariat. These parties were equipped with different ideologies than Congress for the independent India. Despite the challenges, Congress, under the leadership of Gandhiji, Jawahar Lal Nehru, and other eminent leaders, was able to take on the task of challenging the British regime, and succeeded in consolidating the party as well as mobilizing the mass for the greater struggle that was on the cards and pointed toward a new horizon.

The Last Nail in the coffin of the Paper Tiger – The departure from India was precedented on the walls for the white paper tigers. The great depression that swallowed most of the nations of the world, finally compelled them to go into the war. The two hostile blocks i.e., axis and allies were once again facing to each other in the second world war that finally broke out in 1939 of which Britain remained the integral part. In the amidst of war, back in India the situation was confusing and tense, as India was declared an ally without its consent, the act brought the shade of reaction in the masses as well as the leaders. While Indian nationalists showed their discontent and anguish for bringing India into war, on the other hand Muslim league supported the war, but congress was divided. As the war continued, the Britain felt the heat of it on two flanks. Firstly, the deteriorating condition in which Britain itself was poised, and secondly growing dissatisfaction among the Indian troops and the civilian population of India for using them as a shield. Both this situation made them flux with uncertainty.

Therefore, in March 1942, the British government sent a delegation to India that was called the "Cripps Mission" with the sole purpose of forcing the Indian National Congress to reach an agreement on some terms of negotiation. This mission was all set to make a deal with the Congress for their total co-operation during the war, and in return was ready for the distribution of power. The treaty failed, as it was limited to only dominion-status, which wasn't acceptable to the Indian movement. Eventually, Congress and several Indian leaders saw the world war as an opportunity to cash in. But the three major groups, i.e., the Communists, the Muslim League, and the Hindu Mahasabha, didn't support the movement and continued to collaborate with the British Empire. In fact, the Hindu Mahasabha and the Muslim League joined hands to form the provincial governments of Sindh and North-West Frontier Province (NWFP), which later endorsed the partition of India and Pakistan. Interesting, the two poles decided to go into an unholy alliance with the sole motive of spreading the pollution of hatred on religious lines and dismantling harmony, so they could ensure the division of India.

In such a grim atmosphere, Mahatma Gandhi and Congress decided to initiate a new phase of movement against the British, and finally, when the British were severely engaged in the war zone, they gave the call to 'Quit India', i.e., August Kranti on August 9th, 1942. Soon, Gandhi and other leaders were imprisoned, but by then the movement had cross-cut among all sections of society. Although, the movement couldn't last for a long time, it was certainly able to secure two things: 1. It gave utterance to India's anger against imperialism, and 2. It assured the British rulers that the days of imperialist domination could be counted on the fingers.

Finally, the Second World War ended in 1945, and the same year, back in India, to solve the political deadlock, the Wavell Plan was by the British officer, Lord Wavell, and then the very next year, the British prime minister announced a Cabinet Mission which laid the stone for the interim government on September 2nd, 1946. Finally, on 3rd June 1947, power was transferred to two dominion states; India and Pakistan, through the Independence of India Act, 1947.

Indeed, the Indian National Congress neither in nature nor in its program and policies were ever been a monolith, in fact, it was merger of groups with different shades of opinion and beliefs within its fold. Despite reluctant in approach, slowly but gradually has also changed its stance against the British hegemony.

Perhaps, the Indian freedom struggle was one of the greatest mass movements that covered all sections of society as well as every corner of the country. Especially, after 1919, the movement was led by Congress and Gandhi, and was built around the basic notion that the people had to and could play an active role in politics as well as for the liberation of the country. Thus, making a greater impact on the people who moved and mobilized into politics. In fact, from the very beginning, the movement popularized democratic ideas and institutions among the people and promoted them to struggle for the introduction of parliamentary institutions on the basis of popular elections. Perhaps, to ensure the involvement of every Indian, the Congress from its formation urged the British rule to introduce a universal adult franchise.

How weak it may be! But certainly, from the very beginning in 1885, the Indian National Congress did not insist on uniformity of viewpoints or policies, but it allowed the space for dissenting voices within the organization. The congress remained the organization of a vast section of society, who may have endured from the different schools of political thought, but they even found a place in congress. This way, one can say that Congress played a significant role in meshing the different ideologies together with all the tastes of ingredients and serving them to the people to decide the best out of those. We shall continue to analyse more minutely the ideology of Congress in the next chapter, but one thing is certain: it believes that unity and struggle go together.

To the bottom of the lines – one can conclude that the national movement was the legacy of the political comprise, accommodation, and reconciliation of different interests and points of view. Without a single regret, the movement set the highest norms of politics and political behaviour. All the leaders, from Dadabhai Naoroji to Rajendra Prasad and Subhas Chandra Bose, possessed the highest order of moral integrity, and made it possible to mobilize millions. In fact, not only were the leaders absolved, but the cadres were solely devoted to live the national movement.

02

Congress and its Ideology

"Indians today are governed by two different ideologies. Their political ideal set in the preamble of the Constitution affirms a life of liberty, equality and fraternity. Their social ideal embodied in their religion denies them."

(B. R. Ambedkar)

The Indian National Congress, commonly called Congress, will be completing 137 years since its establishment in December 2022. It is a grand old party that has survived itself against all odds, and also witnessed the cherishable moments of politics. A party that began its journey with just seventy-two delegates from various parts of the country in December 1885 to lay the foundation stone for the unending journey. Surely then, no one had even thought that they would be a part of the party that would not only cross the 20th century, but successfully continue its journey into the 21st century. Although presently, when we are inching to celebrate its 137th formation day, the boat of Congress is stuck amidst the political waves and jolting heavily. And for the time being, there is no sign of Samule Taylor Coleridge's albatross in Congress to turn the tide in its favour by breaking the ice.

Is it the political will and charm that have disappeared from the Congress meeting hall? Or is there no faith in the people left in Congress anymore? Or is there something more that needs to be discussed and debated to understand the plight of the oldest party; a party that led the Indian National Movement from the very front; a party that laid the foundation stone of the "New India" in the post-independence; a party that was glorified for its secular stance; it was the party that played a pivotal role in bringing different ideologies together in the constituent assembly to make a unique constitution of India which is endorsed even today not only in India, but several nations of the world admire it for its outstanding achievement. Despite the legacy and glorious past, there was to and fro, which hasn't been talked much about, and also for many years, there has been an atmosphere of silence on the Congress ideology or political views, which continues to show diversion and drifting from the fundamental principles of secularism, socialism, and fraternity. And now, when it is heading toward a drastic decline, it becomes of utmost importance to talk about and understand the positivity and weaknesses of Congress. Nonetheless, it is high time, when even Congressmen need to understand their party ideology, which they emphasize as a "beautiful jewel."

Amalgamation of the Ideologies of East and West – Traditionally, India has had a rich culture of co-existence of diverse ideologies, and Congress isn't far behind in that. This is a land where the principles of Sanatan Dharm co-existed with the theory of charvak or lokayat. We also saw the flourishing of Buddhism and Jainism on this very land that brought new ideas of salvation and meditation to challenge the Brahminical hegemony through the spirit of non-violence in ancient India. Later, at the beginning of the medieval period, the arrival of Turkish and Arabian rulers from the middle-east not only conquered India but also brought and flourished an overseas religious ideology of Islam, which propagated monotheism, or submission to one God. It was also the period when the Bhakti Movement was foreseen in multiple colors and devotional features; it was also the time when Sufis preached about peace and love and ousted the elaborate rituals and codes of Muslim religious scholars. Later in the centuries, we observe the legacy of Kabir to Guru Nanak, who rejected orthodoxy and dogma in religion; whereas, Tulsidas and Surdas believed and practiced on different platforms than the other Bhakti scholars. Yet there was another set of bhakti preachers like Ravi Das and Mirabai of around the sixteenth century who openly challenged the norms of the "upper" castes through bhajans. By the end of the seventeenth century, India was transformed into a bouquet of ideas and thoughts. However, they mainly represented the religious and social culture of the people. Later, in the national movement, we see the amalgamation of traditional thoughts with western political philosophy, which was the backbone of European democracy. Together, the two different ideologies partly interweave to fight against the British Raj.

Early Political Ideologies and Canvases of Pre-Congress Associations – The legacy of multiple ideologies and thoughts didn't die or vanish, rather it voyaged a long way and remained in the heart and soul of the people. Later in the years, it acted as a sublime force to fight against British hegemony; some of that comprehensively took the form of political ideology. These ideologies were further expanded into various shades, i.e., from religious monolithic, western liberal, and extreme religious revolutionary to anarchist and communist revolutionary. One cannot deny or disregard the contribution of socialists, an inevitable force of the Indian National Movement. The mid and the late years of the 19th century witnessed the ideological meshing up of the traditional values and the fostering of liberal thought; an idea more inclined to western culture and western democracy within the educated and elite Indian society, which gradually advanced the essence of nationalism among the common Indians and gave a waking call to liberate the country from not only the British colonial rule, but they equally criticized and wanted an end to the Zamindari system and old orthodox traditional values. Both the groups were distinct from each other in aims as well as objectives. The extreme religious revolutionary wanted to reconstruct India on the values of Hindu religion principles and used Hindu Gods and Goddesses and traditional symbols to boost religious supremacy and mobilize people, especially Hindus, from the upper caste to fight against the British. Certainly, this ideology is devoid of all the other forces that were interested in ending the tyranny of the British Raj. To counter this, the Muslims organized themselves separately, and finally formed the Muslim League in 1907. Bhimrao Ambedkar, another prominent and eminent leader of the national movement, was harshly critical of the upper caste dominance and idealistic thought within the Congress. Earlier, the decade of the 1870s can be marked as a turning point, when several new associations under the leadership of middle-class background professionals started twinkling on the Indian horizon. Most of these associations were dominated by the urbans who replaced the older associations; some of the notable ones included the Indian League, and the Indian

Association in Calcutta; the Bombay Presidency Association, Madras Mahajan Sabha or Poorna Sarvajanik Sabha, were the major associations that ignited a process of political change from the 1870s onwards.

Thanks to the print media that played a significant role in spreading the atmosphere in the latter half of the 19th century, the organizations of professionals increasingly started to acquire the character of quasi-political associations. The legal profession, like the judiciary and educational system, became the breeding ground for a dissident intelligentsia. In fact, the dissident nationalist managed to penetrate a certain kind of nationalist consensus on important political issues by the virtue of print media. Indeed, the spread of print media helped in the expansion of the politics of associations in the form of public expression, which, in the fear of yet another mutiny, was rigorously censored by Lord Lytton under the Vernacular Press Act of 1878, in order to control the percolation of anti-British sentiments in the regions where the newspapers were expanding their reach. One can say that the despotic character of the British Raj also contributed to the emergence of a liberal critique by the early nationalists.

The series of arbitrary events and actions during the British brute rule started to consolidate the Indians politically, socially, and ideologically to mobilize them against the grave rule of the British. Indeed, one thing is for sure for any political wing to survive itself – is having faith in certain kinds of ideological principles. And Congress was no different from others. Perhaps, the emergence of Congress in 1885 was the culmination and accumulation of all different kinds of ideologies into a single fold for the broader cause, and that was to mobilize all sections of the Indian population to fight against colonial rule. In this chapter, we shall try to understand the changing phases of the Congress ideology, and what its impact has been on the overall socio-political landscape of India? Of course, at this juncture when Congress is facing the worst phase in its history. Thus, it becomes important to dissect the ideological causes behind the dismal condition of Congress.

Congress as a Centrist Party – The ride of the Congress as a party to lead the national movement in the first phase (1885–1947) was the era of the sacrifices and devotion of congressmen under the leadership of Mahatma Gandhi. The declaration of independence and thereafter the construction of "New India" (1947–1963) was a new challenge, later India entered into the new phase; it was the phase of India's political and economic transformational age, which remained interesting. In a long journey, however, Congress always proclaimed itself to be a centrist party, which means a party neither a believer in left nor right politics. Indeed, the Indian National Congress has never been a monolith in its opinions and beliefs. Nevertheless, since its formation and in the coming decades, Congress was a party that swung between the spirit of Swami-bhakti and urged for progressivism, but later in the years, this party gradually but steadily changed into an inclusive movement of broad-based multi-classes.

Though Congress started its political journey with a demand for reform within the British Raj, in the years to come, the political vision of Congress crossed the bars of preaching and praising the British and, in fact, wasn't limited to just opposing colonial rule, rather it developed a strong ideological base, which one can regard as an anti-imperialist vision.

It worked and capitalized on its vision, which was enrooted in the ideological view of a secular, republican, democratic, and civil libertarian society. In fact, it emphasized the need for economic and political transformation based on the principles of social equality. Interestingly, this vision is still relevant within the rank and files of Congress.

While discussing the ideology of Congress or Indian National Congress, one can traverse its journey into five-folds; that is, from the formation of the Congress in 1885, the journey crosses seven seas of India's politics. In this long journey, Congress has foregone with the single dominant party in India to its pathetic downhill journey in recent years. Despite the fact, one can say that Congress ideology hasn't been totally wiped out; it is a vibrant and living ideology for millions of Indians. An ideology that advocates the unification of the country and its people to live together. Let's diagnose the ideology in bits to understand the ideological strength and weaknesses of the oldest party in India from its early-stage formation to the present day.

The Early Congress – The story of Congress ideology begins with the formation, a party constituted of seventy-two delegates to begin in 1885 with the sole aim of achieving some power in British India for Indians. Indeed, it was the party that synthesized the feelings of nationalism in a wider section of society. For Congress, it was an early stage, but it based its ideology on national unity, social inclusion, and self-reliance. These principles became effective in making a strong and united India and setting a goal to achieve independence in the later years. The Congress believed and remained volatile for the equal rights and opportunities for every Indian, regardless of their caste or religion. It viewed and advocated the principle of self-reliance, so that Indians wouldn't rely on the compassion of others but develop India in accordance to their spirit of thought. Later, this principle was further strengthened by Gandhian philosophy, where he urged "Swaraj" and advocated self-reliance.

However, the early Congress, as foreseen, advanced in the shadow of moderators and their ideology, who were much influenced by Western political ideas and practices. Their philosophy, perhaps, emphasized the need for Congress to believe in the principles of

1   Dignity of the individual
2   Rights to freedom for individuals
3   Equality for all regardless of their respective caste, creed, or sex.

Furthermore, the liberal philosophy guided the Congress to oppose the autocratic British government, demanding the rule of law and equality before the law and advocating secularism. But for this, moderate leaders only humbly requested the British rulers for two reasons:

1. Most moderate leaders had an abiding attachment to the British way of life, a belief in the British sense of justice and fair play, and a deep sense of gratitude towards British rulers. They believed that it was their relationship with British rule and English education that had given them the opportunity to be exposed to modern ideas such as liberty, equality, democracy, and the dignity of the individual.

2. They were also aware that the Indian National Congress was still a budding organization and therefore were not

willing to incur the wrath of the British rulers. In a nutshell, the early Congress disfavored a direct confrontation with the British Raj.

Nevertheless, for the duration of sixty-odd years, Congress remained a prime facia in fighting the anti-colonial struggle and an advocate of Swaraj in India. This was the phase when several shades of ideologies also emerged within Congress itself. Among them, the most prominent were the radicals. But the rise of radicals wasn't sudden. Indeed, it had garnered its position since the 1857 mutiny, and later, various international events also gave impetus to the growth of radicalism in India, especially by the end of the 19th century. The early years of the 20th century witnessed conflict within the Congress between the two vibrant forces of the time, i.e., the moderates and the radicals. Although the conflict arose on the issue of the mode of action against the British hegemony, as they wanted radical action and emphasized the active involvement of the mass in the agitations. Both wanted to initiate the 'Swaraj', but the action plan differentiated from one another. The pride in India's ancient heritage remained the thrust of their aims.

The emerging and spreading of right and left ideologies in the 1920s brought Congress and its ideology under critical scrutiny by the patronage of other ideologies. But under the Mahatma Gandhi charisma, Congress was comprehensively able to garner all the political, ideological, and social weeds that emerged all through the movement, and remained a sublime force throughout the national movement struggle despite obstacles from inside as well as from external forces.

The Constituent Assembly and Congress – Another journey of Congress starts with the formation of the Indian constituent assembly and making a constitution for the beloved land and its people, and thereafter, taking India to a new height from the dark ages of British rule. But how was it to be done? Independence of India didn't only shower joy, but nevertheless, pathetic sorrows also. The partition of India and Pakistan, and then the sleuthing of innocent people on both sides, was gruesome and beyond the wildest dreams of civilized society. Another blessing in disguise was the princely states, which were not ready at any cost to be part of Indian territory. It was a challenge for the leaders then to ensure that they boarded the same ship by all means. It was significant for India's integration, and finally the ruined economy by the British rulers. Some of the testimonies that narrate the dismal macabre of the prevailing conditions at the time of India's independence.

In several ways, India's independence was a hot potato for its leaders, and therefore, it was a challenge for them to bring back the hopes of the people and lost glory for India. Once again, It was the Congress and its leadership that took the burden on their shoulders to harness the best in the worst of times. In the early period of post-independence, Jawahar Lal Nehru and Sardar Vallabhbhai Patel, the two architects of Azaad India, not only played an immense role in the making of the Indian Constitution, although their role in the constituent assembly was never direct, but acted as a shield to rescue the country from all odds.

It was a period when initiatives were taken to establish democracy, and further enhanced to establish socialism and constructive nation-building. The reflections of Congress and Mahatma Gandhi were clearly reflected in the Indian constitution. Being a centrist party, Congress's policies predominantly reflected balanced positions that included secularism, egalitarianism, and social stratification. These principles existed in policies and programs like equal opportunity, welfare of weaker sections, and special rights to minorities, and also in the strong support for mixed economy for many decades of the 20th century. But at the same time, the pulses of ideological and economic diversion were also realized.

To Whom Congress Concerns – Ideology is the systematic scheme and process of ideas about the social, economic, and political life processes of society, which political parties adhere to and proceed in their journey. Indeed, a bundle of distinct and unambiguous ideas and creeds makes for both, i.e., unity and cohesion within the party and brings the members under its control. Congress was an organization that emerged in the shadow of elite middle class intellectuals that propounded the theory of peaceful political action and public interest and public protest. To begin, one can say that in a society where the existence of multifarious religious and cultural manifestations, ethnic diversities, and economic higher-ups and lower-downs echelon, Congress on the stage of politics played the role of a pluralist, flexible, and open-ended organization, and is still in the same attire.

Indeed, the ideology of a party plays a decisive role and is often reflected in the policies and programs of a party. So do the same criteria equally fit for Congress also, and indeed, for several years, every single word inscribed in its ideology has thrived in the programs and policies of the party. But having co-opted the ideological shades of the right-center-left from the Nehru period wasn't going to have a cake walk in the future. Perhaps, in the Nehru era, the party as well as the leadership were in equilibrium and equally strong, as no major opposition threat was there to challenge the supremacy of Nehru and the ideology of Gandhi, either internally or from other parties. Gandhi's assassination by the right-wing forces brought the rightest ideology into feeble condition, causing them to raise questions about the stalwart leadership of Nehru. Whereas, the Communist Party of India almost surrendered itself to the British in the Second World War when it decided to support allies against the axis. Thus, by refraining itself from the 'Quit India' call of Congress, eventually the CPI dug its own grave. Further, a section of the CPI leadership admired Nehruvian socialism. All these factors played a crucial role in muting voices from both flanks of the ideologies that existed within Congress itself.

The demise of Jawaharlal Nehru and the two wars, Indo-China and India-Pakistan, and growing unemployment and poverty added fuel as well as strength among the opposition leaders and party to wake up from hibernation. The decade of the 70s of the 20th century observed tough ideological conflict between Indira, a pillar of Gandhian principles, and the right-wing leadership in the Congress, and finally, subsequent expulsion paved the way for the center to pursue the left policies of nationalization and speed up the development of the public sector as the backbone of the Indian economy. Though, this event made Indira the heavyweight leader of her time, her charismatic leadership also weakened the party rank and file because of her authoritative decisions and maintaining the policy of single party dominance.

Nevertheless, the reshuffling of ideology continued, and as a result, Congress's programs and policies also kept on changing in bits and pieces. The party leadership embarked upon the modest Gandhian principles, but shadows of respective leaderships brought diversion in its ideology. At times, Congress seemed to be close to getting closer to communal politics to seek the support of majority Hindus, and at other times it looked closer to Muslims. On economic policies, the party always claimed to be pro-people, but consequently saw the party landing on a very different horizon of new economic policy. It makes very little difference what excuses they are compelled to give to satisfy the people.

Thus, the change in policies flooded several questions and compelled me to think and react about the Congress and the Congressmen: Do they truly understand the ideology the Congress upholds? Is it remained the same party that propounded to hold the view of socialism, secularism, or believed in the amalgamation of moderate or radical, left or right or center, or can we still trust it to be a centrist party? Indeed, in the last few decades, Congress hasn't been the same face that stood for the downtrodden, underprivileged class of society. Deliberate changes have been seen in the stances of Congress from its earlier days. Sometimes it appears to be actively pursuing neo-liberalism and sitting in the lap of corporator families (though it expresses the implementation with human-face). Other times, the same Congress would find itself close to the right-wing fanatic forces; in 1984, the anti-Sikh riots and in 1992, the demolishment of Babri Masjid, set a narrative of the pro-Hindu stance of the Congress, where it remained a silent spectator of the terrible chopping and eliminating of minorities and brought an end to the long-lasting heritage and culture of diverse unity by not protecting the minorities, are some of the mind-blowing incidents that forced a rethinking of the Congress philosophy. Very interestingly, Congress's ideology did go through grave changes in the economic sphere when she made a murky announcement of supporting economic reform in 1991, thus paving the path for liberalization, globalization, and strategic disinvestment. Surely, this act was an avalanche of its ideology. Now, it is the right time where Congress should prove itself on the issues related to the social and economic spheres whether it is a party for the poor, as it often proclaims through its programs and ideology. Though the facts reveal that, via versa, it had conjured power for a good time after India's Independence.

Dynastic Succession: A Power Lust or Compulsion – Ideology, whether good or bad, serves and expands only in the guidance of efficient leaders who believe in certain thoughts. The Gandhian principles are admired even today only because there have been leaders and cadres who made their efforts for their comprehensive and continuous propagation in theories as well as in practice. Several parties and leaders, as well as, now and then, a section of society, keep harping and scolding the Gandhi or Nehru families for promoting nepotism in politics. Definitely, this argument is like two sides of the coin, and therefore cannot be answered in just black and white. As the history of Congress reveals the basic fact that it had never been a party of one ideology, in fact, it consisted of leaders and cadres that belonged or believed in different ideologies; in such a situation, there has been a threat of domination of a particular and peculiar type of ideology.

However, it has been seen and experienced again and again that the Gandhi family stood more firmly than others when the clouds hovered over the Gandhian principles and the ideology of Congress or be it the internal affairs of the party. Undoubtedly, the family has always been volatile and aggressive to safeguard its ideology from any threat of dismantling. Despite the allegation of dictatorial ruler, Indira Gandhi stood firmly to protect the Congress from the malign and escapist right-wing leaders who shrewdly termite the ideology of Congress. Sonia Gandhi in the first and second decade garnered the Congress's support from all kinds of obstacles from the rising right-wing at the national level, and now Rahul Gandhi plays a pivotal role in bringing Nehruvian socialism to the forefront of politics. Thus, dynastic politics for the Gandhi family isn't a choice but a compulsion to avoid further deterioration of Congress ideology and the principles of Gandhi. As it is the only party that has kept the legacy of Gandhi's thought and Nehruvian socialism alive despite the fact that the right-wing, BJP has overshadowed the loving, affectionate and nationalistic ideology of the Congress party, this is only for a while.

In the long journey of almost 137 years since its formation in December, 1885, Congress has seen phases of diversion in its ideologies and principles, whether they be social, political, or economic issues. During the national movement, under the efficient guidance of Gandhi, the party was able to fight all ideologies that were against the unity of the country. But later on, in the post-independence period to present, Congress partly lost the grip on its ideology mainly for two definite reasons – socio-economic situation, where Congress failed to cope with the situation, and secondly, in certain periods the right-wing leaders within Congress acted against the principles of Congress, which led toward the decline of Congress. A party which was once known for its strong leadership, structure, and ideological agenda of a welfare state for the poor, has now been highjacked by the BJP. Nevertheless, Congress still holds the strong legacy of Gandhian ideals and values. But any legacy, no matter how strong it is, becomes irrelevant if it is not nurtured and developed continuously. Thus, it is the responsibility of the current congress to not only strengthen the legacy that they have obtained from the past leaders, but to go ahead and make some creative changes as per the present circumstances. Without a doubt, in the post-independence period, Congress devoted itself to creating a liberal country. A glimpse of it could be measured in the framing of the Indian Constitution. Further, it could be scaled through agricultural reforms, economic reforms, and educational reforms.

Indeed, the foundational work of Congress remained strong, but at the same time, it has been the omnibus party that hindered or put a dent in its ideology. Whether the omnibus culture will advance the party or not in the present political scenario, where the BJP is much ahead of Congress in practice and ideology, is yet to be seen. Thus, what should be the next step to advance its politics? Indeed, advancement in politics means gaining political power, and political power can be harnessed only when the party makes efforts to counter the right-wing surge in the broad spectrum of secular politics and goes ahead with taking the ideology of Congress among the wider section of the people; especially in the communities that remain the backbone of its politics. But, do Congress and its soldiers harbor any ideology or thought process and take that among the massive section of society? However, some of the rebuilding of the party organization has commenced by Rahul Gandhi, the former President of Congress, but still needs hard work, determination, and passion not only by a single leader, but more importantly, a major leadership should be a part of such events of connecting with people, and a large-scale ideological training of party workers from top to bottom must be mandatory for all the Congressmen.

To conclude As Rahul claimed, "the beautiful jewel" in the Congress ideology, no wonder the Congress ideology still represents the heritage and culture of India. Indian isn't a fence of a homogeneous society, but has a diverse social order in terms of religion, culture, language, etc. Such a society can never be woven into one kind of thought and practice. In such versatile diversity, the accommodation of several identities is a daunting task for any political party. Certainly, the party too needs to garner the elements that are earnestly able to advance its ideology according to the time and situation. And despite the worst phase, Congress has the ideas and values of an ideology that can serve as a bridge to achieve political success.

03

Role of Congress in Building the Nation (1950-1975)

"There cannot be firmly established political state unless there is a teaching body with definitely recognized principles. If the child is not taught from infancy that he ought to be a republican or a monarchist, a Catholic or a free-thinker, the state will not constitute a nation; it will rest on uncertain and shifting foundations; and it will be constantly exposed to disorder and change."

– Napoleon I

Nation-building is an aspect and a process of uniting the people of the state together into a well-functioning, good governing, well-dignified and unified nation, where the political, social, economic, and cultural institutions develop in the strict vigilance of the state power. It enhances an enthusiasm among the people to participate in the process of modernization, development and socio-economic construction of a nation, with the zeal of nationalism. In other words, nation building is referred to the phase of construction and restructuring the identity of a Nation by using the power of the state. Nation-building goes through simultaneous process of adding brick over brick to advance the nation in the following aspects and then simultaneously make each of the pillar i.e., state, people, democracy, economy, social and government stronger as well as versatile.

The process of nation building in India, can be traced from the year 1950, with a very important event of enforcing the Indian Constitution on the twenty-sixth day of the first month. It was a long awaited and cherished moment for all Indians who longed for a long time to have their own Constitution; a constitution that provided them the dignity to live with others on the basic principle of equality. Equality meant walking on the democratic values enhanced by equal status in all spheres of life without discrimination. In fact, the Indian Constitution provided its people with the right to achieve power for themselves without being biased on the basis of religion, caste, gender, or economic ground through electoral politics. However, the achievement wasn't a day's effort. This Constitution was shaped in the company of many eminent intellectual, political, and social activists who were involved in different kinds of professions, believed in different ideologies, and belonged to diverse social orders and geographical features of the country. Despite their differences, they came together to frame one of the most beautiful and practical constitutions. Each and every person who was part of the Constituent Assembly was ambiguous about taking India toward a unique democracy that suited Indians' diverse cultures, languages, and customs and traditions. This, definitely, isn't the product of a day or a few years, but is a historical process. When we recall the memories, we need to go deep into the roots of nationhood, and for that, we definitely go beyond the Gazebo for the truth, and from there upon, turn the pages of the Indian National Movement struggle, which shaped many things more than the Independence struggle. And that is why, despite immense cultural diversity, certain strands of a common cultural heritage had developed that not only knitted people of different folds together but also gave them a sense of oneness. There is no doubt that the national movement played a pivotal role in wielding Indians both politically and emotionally and further integrating them into 'a common framework of political identity and loyalty."

The leaders of the national movement were very well aware of the fact that the making of a nation was a prolonged and continuous process, and this had to face challenges as well as interruption. And one disruption had already taken place at the time of the declaration of independence of India, when we witnessed the division of India into two nations, India and Pakistan, and that too was in the ugliest form; i.e., the religious line, which led toward the massacre of millions from both sides of the declared border; rape of women and looting were the horrors of those days. The holocaust moved the leaders of the founders of the Indian republic to pursue more toward unifying India and for national integration. In fact, the leaders saw the preservation and consolidation of India as a major challenge after its independence. Jawaharlal Nehru expressed his worries in 1952: "the most important factor, the overriding factor, is the unity of India'. In fact, the other parties also showed their benevolent affection for the same.

Nehru to Indira and the dream of modern India – The stage was set and so were the players, who were ready for their performance in the first ever democratic electoral politics of India after the official declaration of India to be a democratic republican country. The declaration of the Indian Constitution was the accumulation of the mixed emotional responses. India had already lost the iconic leader and messiah of non-violence,

Mahatma Gandhi, because of his firm stand for Hindu-Muslim unity. The coward right-wing opportunistic leader, who never ever took responsibility for the heinous murder, though it is an open secret that this force continues to celebrate the assassination of Gandhi as a mark of pride and courage till the present day for the Hindus.

After the assassination of the father of the nation, Mahatma Gandhi, Jawaharlal Nehru became the forefront leader and the ideologue of the Congress. His thoughts were the ideology of the Congress, and they continue to overshadow all others. Despite the fact that he was bent toward socialism but never imitated it in the copy and paste form, one can say that there was an amalgamation of Gandhian principles and socialism as per the requirements of Indian society.

In an atmosphere of trust and faith in Congress and its leader, India went into its first parliamentary general election. It was a colossal exercise that took place between October 25, 1951 and February 21, 1952, where a large number of the Indian populace voted for the introduction of the universal adult franchise. The election was organized to bring an end to the Constituent Assembly, as its sole motive had already been fulfilled with the declaration of the Indian Constitution. The first election witnessed a land slide victory for Nehru and Congress, i.e., 364 out of 479 constituencies were bagged by the Congressmen. The only other party was the CPI, which secured 16 seats, and remained runner-up. While the Socialist Party (SOC) led by Jayaprakash Narayan and Ram Manohar Lohiya was able to secure twelve Lok Sabha seats, the Indian National Congress also garnered an invincible victory in a majority of the State Assembly elections, nevertheless, these two events not only strengthened the leadership of Nehru but also paved the way for a Nehruvian era in India. In fact, the Congress's dominion glared for a long time after the first general election, winning eleven of the fourteen general elections until its collapse in 2014, when the country's tide turned in favor of the BJP under the leadership of Narendra Modi. The dramatic collapse of the Congress we shall discuss in the coming chapters.

Political analysts like Rajni Kothari, in his book "Politics in India", define the Nehruvian era as the dominance of a one-party system. According to him, "A competitive party system has two competing parts which have dissimilar roles, i.e., parties of pressure and parties of consensus." Nehru's Congress or the Congress of the 50s and 60s could be identified as the party of consensus, and that is why it would be considered a dominant party with an obligation towards nation-building in all spheres. In fact, it was the time when the Indian political system emphasized the modernization, development of infrastructure, establishing national unity and integrity, and generating employment by emphasizing industrialization and the advancement of agriculture. For sustainable economic growth, Jawaharlal Nehru emphasized a socialistic mode of system in the form of a mixed economy. How important was this new model of economy then, we shall discuss later, but for sure, certainly these policies harvested back-to-back victories for Nehru-led Congress in the years 1952, 1957, and 1962 Lok Sabha elections. During this long period, the Congress party system worked in a copybook manner from the top leadership to the local level. There was overlap between the executive and legislative wings, but the work profile was clearly demarcated. It was done mainly for the proper untied functioning and to serve the constitutional propriety with full respect.

The thrust of the socialistic approach could be seen very clearly in the early post-independence India. Among the many was the implementation of the Five-Year Plan on July 9, 1951, to achieve the goal of transiting India from colonial India to modern and democratic India. The Five-Year Plan remained the backbone of Congress's developmental programs till the end of 2014 in the smooth functioning of an economic program. The ray of a new sun on a new day of a new year brought an end to the Five-Year Plan and the beginning of the NITI Aayog. The prime motives are growth, employment, self-reliance, and social justice.

The first four five-year plans emphasized the development of basic structures like irrigation and energy, agriculture and community development, transport and communication, industrialization, health services, education, and employment. As the early 50s witnessed the turmoil of influx of refugees, food scarcity, poverty, and mounting inflation, and for all these, some sought equilibrium was required to balance the economy that the British regime had ruined. The other important issue was building infrastructure, and this could have been done at a rapid pace only when India had thought and implemented the policy of industrialization, especially in heavy industries. In fact, Nehru called "industry" the temple of modern India.

Growth of Infrastructure, Health and School Education (1951 to 1966)

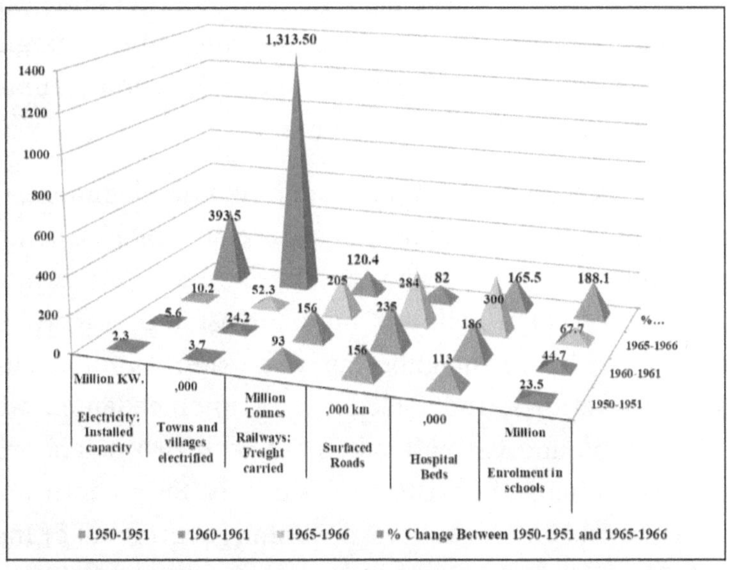

Source: J. Bhagwati and P. Desai, India: Planning fir Industrialization, London, 1970, pg. 74

Further, in 1955, the Congress shifted more towards socialism while declaring the pattern of society as its primary goal. The backbone of Indian economy, agriculture was going through unprecedented crisis. as a result, it was throwing out the peasants from the dependency on agriculture and compelled them to search other ways for their livelihood. The impact of the crisis wasn't stable to this only, in fact, shortage of foodgrain made Indian government rely on the USA for foodgrain, especially wheat. In such circumstances, there was an essential need to boost the agriculture, and this could have happened by using the new and latest technology in the production. Finally, the Congress government decided to implement the New Agricultural Strategy in the late 60s and early 70s to boost the agriculture. This strategy was known as the Green Revolution, though, in the early days, it able to increase the earning of the big farmers, but at the same time, this was also the process of de-peasantization of the marginal and poor peasant, which eventually led toward agrarian unrest and revolt in many parts of the country.

The ruling Congress initiated the policy of non-alignment, i.e., sided away from the bipolar two superpower blocks, i.e., the United States of America and the Soviet Union. Furthermore, it adopted a foreign policy of mutual trust and peaceful co-existence with the neighboring countries. Unfortunately, despite the efforts, India faced three unprecedented wars in 1961, 1965 and thereafter in 1971 with two neighboring countries, China and Pakistan, respectively. But in both wars, despite the odd circumstances, the union government of India led by Congress under the leadership of Jawaharlal Nehru and later Mrs. Indira Gandhi responded with courage and wisdom, giving a fitting reply despite the limited resources.

The Congress in the first two decades of the post-independence period also played a crucial role in establishing institutions of higher education, that included All India Institute of Medical Sciences (AIIMS), Indian Institutes of Management (IIM), Indian Institutes of Technology (IIT), National Institutes of Technology (NIT) etc. In 1961, the National Council of Educational Research and Training (NCERT) was established for research and awareness programs in the field of education and scientific approach among students. In fact, early Congress also played an immense role in promoting art, culture, and all-round development by helping to establish the Lalit Kala Academy and the Sahitya Academy. Even Jawaharlal

Nehru had deep concern about education, and that is why he outlined his commitment in the Five-Year Plans to guarantee free and compulsory primary education to all Indian children below the age of fourteen. To reduce the poverty, the Scheduled Castes and the Scheduled Tribes Commission was set up to implement welfare scheme for the underprivileged communities. Linguistic division and discrimination were the hurdle in the unification of the country, so to reduce the commission was set up with the prime motive to reduce the hostile tendency between Hindi and non-Hindi speaking states. In 1961, the National Integration Council was set up primarily to control the communal flare.

Growth in Technical Education (1951 to 1966)

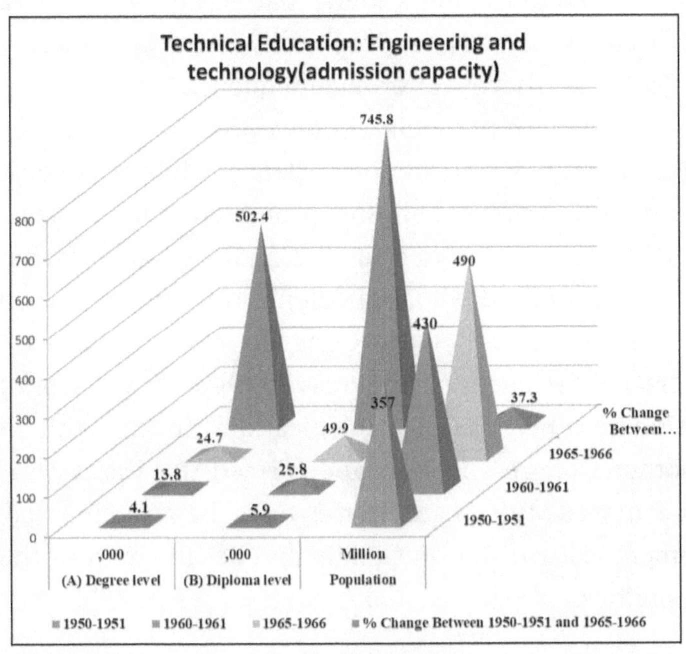

Source: J. Bhagwati and P. Desai, India: Planning fir Industrialization, London, 1970, pg. 74

Era of Struggle and Unity within and Outside the Congress – After the assassination of Mahatma Gandhi, Nehru was the only leader with a dynamic personality, a vision, and a mass-scale mobilization of people behind him. His words were prophetic within the rank and files of Congress, but the glaring impact was also seen among the common Indians. It doesn't mean that none of the challenging voices existed. Definitely, Nehru was being challenged within the party, but it was feeble. In fact, many of the dissenting voices that were raised against Congress were from the rank and files of Congress. Later, many of these leaders separated themselves from the Congress to form their own party or remained critical to Nehru's policies. The other factor that created a rift among the Congress leadership was the ideological differences with Mahatma Gandhi. The leaders, like Jayaprakash Narayan, Lohiya, and Acharya Narendra Dev, eventually separated from the Congress shortly after independence, and formed the Socialist Party. In particular, Lohiya preached and abided by the Gandhian principle of non-violence, while JP advocated a more militant approach. Another prominent leader of Congress was Kripalani, who was a staunch Gandhian, and remained an integral part of the Civil Disobedience movement, also served as general-secretary of the Congress from 1934-1945 and was elected president of Congress in 1946. He departed from the Congress because of ideological differences with Nehru and other Congress leaders and formed the Kisan Mazdoor Praja Party (KMPP). Later in the years, he also emerged as a vehement critic of Indira Gandhi and became part of the up-field politics.

The most prominent parties that were challenging and emerging as threats to the Congress and Gandhian principles, as well as Nehruvian thoughts, were the Akhil Bhartiya Hindu Mahasabha (HMS), Akhil Bhartiya Ram Rajya Parishad (RRP), and All India Bhartiya Jan Sangh (BJS). All these parties favored and supported the "Hindu Rashtra' theory, and in fact, dreamt of India's being a Hindu Rashtra and not a secular nation, as the Indian Constitution proclaims to itself. HMS also had the support of prominent leaders like Madan Mohan Malviya and Lala Lajpat Rai. In fact, most of these and their ideologues abstained from the civil disobedience movement, HMS went ahead to form coalition governments with its arch opponent, the Muslim League, and supported the demand for the partition of the country. The prominent leaders of the right-wing fanatic parties were Shyama Prasad Mukherjee, Keshav Baliram Hedgewar, Harharanand 'Swami' Karpatri, and Savarkar. Most of these leaders and parties later joined the Bharatiya Jan Sangh (BJS), to form a united platform to fight a pitched battle against Congress and its ideology under the shadow of the Rashtriya Swayamsevak Sangh (RSS), which was formed in 1925. Later in the years, the Jan Sangh registered itself as the Bhartiya Janta Party in 1980 to spread the ideology of RSS. Now the same party is a major ruling party in many states and union since 2014. It is interesting that many of the leaders and cadres of right-wing parties also snipped in Congress and on many occasions polluted the ideology of Congress and remained a threat to the various fundamental principles of the Indian Constitution.

In the years following the independence of India, the Congress remained a sandwich party, crushing in between right-wing ideology and left-wing, Marxist ideology. The Communist Party of India, which supported the Britishers in the Second World War, was against the Quit India call of Gandhi, later propounded itself to follow in the footsteps of Congress. Although the CPI played a pivotal role in mobilizing the workers and the peasants, apart from the intelligentsia class, it also encouraged the armed struggle against the landlords in some patches of the country, but the frequent changes of stance made it little more than a rolling stone in Indian politics. Perhaps one of the prominent leaders and the secretary of the party, M. N. Roy, was finally disillusioned by the CPI politics and joined Congress in 1936 with his followers, but the honeymoon was short-lived, say nearly four years. Further, a split within the CPI gave rise to and gradually formed the Communist Party of India (Marxist). Besides the CPI, there were smaller left parties like the Revolutionary Communist Party of India (RCPI), Bolshevik Party of India (BPI). Another force, though not very strong, was founded by B. R. Ambedkar in 1942, the All India Scheduled Castes' Federation (SCF). This party basically consolidated itself in Maharashtra and worked against the domination of caste and capitalist structures in India, and for the rights of Dalits in India. Later in 1957, after the demise of B. R. Ambedkar, he was succeeded by the Republican Party of India (RPI), which Ambedkar himself attempted to establish in 1956 after quitting the ministerial post as a law minister of the union government of India in the year 1951 after the dispute over the Hindu Code Bill which was dropped by the cabinet because of the immense pressure the Hindu right-wing organizations and leaders.

So broadly speaking, Congress wasn't going to have an easy walk, despite the fact it was able to bag a huge majority in the first general election. Indeed, the tug-a-war continued between the different rival ideological camps for the lust of power and also led India according to their own respective ideologies. On several occasions, some of the leaders from Congress resigned or were ousted by the leadership, and in many cases, the split had been observed in the Congress during the first quarter years after independence. In a nutshell, there were a cacophony of grievances, but amidst of infighting and external pressure, Congress, under the leadership of Jawaharlal Nehru, was able to pave the way for the socialistic Indian model, which was very different from the Soviet model of socialism, but opened the door of economic development and advanced toward modern India.

Back to electoral politics, the two other general elections were held for the Lok Sabha and state assemblies in 1957 and 1962. In both, the voter turnout improved and Congress continued to gain an overwhelmingly majority in Lok Sabha. The two who stood as enemy camps in practice and in ideology, i.e., right and left, couldn't pose a serious threat to Congress. However, able to make inroads into the Congress hegemony in a few states, such as Kerala, the Communists were able to seize power in Kerala by forming their own government in 1957. Indeed, it was the first Communist government other than the socialist Soviet Union and China that had come into power in a state of a country that didn't hold the Marxist ideology, where the mode of production wasn't classically fitted the socialist approach of Marxism, nor had the rule of proletarian dictatorship. In the era of Nehru, despite the dominance of the Congress party, the role of the opposition also strengthened, as Nehru obliged the opposition with respect and was responsive to their criticism. Indeed, Congress wasn't a monolithic party and encompassed within itself several political and ideological trends that existed in and out of the party. But the black patch on the democratic value of the Congress government was the dismissal of the democratically elected Communist government of Kerala and imposition of Presidential rule.

For a short time after the demise of Jawaharlal Nehru in 1964, though, Lal Bahadur Shastri, a staunch Gandhian, was a non-controversial leader from Uttar Pradesh who had remained a part of Nehru's cabinet for many years, was unanimously chosen as the leader of the Congress parliamentary party and became the country's next Prime Minister. He remained Prime Minister from 1964 to 1966. Though Congress couldn't get much contribution from Shastri ji, at the time when he headed the country, India was still recovering from the economic ruin of the war with China, failed monsoons, and drought in various parts of the country, which resulted in a severe food crisis. These problems present a grave challenge. Besides, India faced a war with Pakistan in 1965, which rubbed salt to the problems. Lal Bahadur Shastri took the challenge and continued to foster the ideology of Congress. In fact, to resolve the challenges, he authored the famous slogan 'Jai Jawan, Jai Kisan'. Unfortunately, his Prime Ministership came to a sudden end on January 10, 1966, when he suddenly expired in Tashkent.

The year 1967 was a landmark in Indian political as well as electoral history. Earlier, we came across the dominancy of Congress as a political and social force. Nonetheless, the act and the words of Congress were prophetic words for not only the rank and files of Congress, but the ordinary Indians too. Though in no way, one can come to the conclusion that everything was going well for the Congress. Unexpectedly, the Congress was facing inner conflict as well as outrage from external forces also. But Nehru, who was a stalwart leader not only in the Congress but also for the opposition, thus left those forces with little choice to raise their voices, and in some circumstances, if they raised their voices, they had very little impact on the common people. But gradually, with the rise of unemployment, poverty, inflation, etc., the people's dream also shattered in disillusionment and resentment. Without any reluctancy and argument, one can very firmly stand for the need of the Congress government in the early stage of free India, which was totally messed up by the British rule, but ironically, its overarching dominance sowed seeds of self-weakening, which later in the years blasted in the form of split and division of the Congress into several branches, as well as the 1967 election under the leadership of Indira Gandhi, jolted the Congress at both the national and state levels. Somehow, Congress managed to get the majority in the Lok Sabha, but with its ever-lowest tally of seats and share of votes since 1952. Many of the stalwarts of the Congress lost their own seats.

The situation for Congress was even more vulnerable in seven states where it lost a majority, and another two states where a defection law prevented it from forming a government. It was the time in the history of Indian electoral politics when the coalition phenomenon came into the picture. However, most of the non-congress coalition governments didn't survive for long. The sudden decline in populace support can be traced to two different narratives of the political analysts; one that takes into account the possible roots of desire and lust for power in some leaders within the leaders of Congress, and the second narrative takes us to another view point that is related to policy matter. Was it the growing crisis in the country that resulted in aggressive movement in the 1960s and 70s?

Definitely, to reach the root cause of the resentment within and outside of Congress, we need to investigate thoroughly the social, political, and economic causes.

After the death of Jawaharlal Nehru and Lal Bahadur Shastri, Congress was encircled with grave challenges. The crisis had been erupting in the form of smoke since the very early years of the 60s, but was managed by experienced leaders like Jawaharlal Nehru and then Shastri, along with other Congress leaders. Interestingly enough, during the entire period of Congress Party government conflict, a contradiction between theory and practice was clearly manifest in Nehru's political discourse, which left a deep impact on the country's emerging political system in the later years.

After the death of Lal Bahadur Shastri, the foremost challenge that Congress faced was political succession. There had been intense competition between the two stalwart leaders for the prime ministership post. The Indira was backed by the senior leaders of the party, but the decision wasn't unanimous. Finally, the contest between Indira and Morarji Desai was resolved by the means of a secret ballot, where Indira was able to achieve victory. It was the first occasion since the beginning of electoral politics that an intense competition was seen. In fact, it was a sign of the maturity of India's democracy.

Another was the economic situation, which had triggered By now, there has been widespread protest in various parts of the country against the increase in the price of essential commodities, food scarcity, unemployment, etc. The Congress saw these protests as a law-and-order problem, and not an expression of the people's problems. As a result, public bitterness and popular unrest started shaping against the system and the constitution, which eventually led to armed agrarian struggles with the formation of the CPI (ML), led by Charru Mazumdar, who believed in the counter surgency against the state to establish the democracy of the working and peasant class through protracted guerrilla warfare. The main stream political parties also couldn't have isolated themselves from the opportunity to garner space in public protests and pressurize the Congress government. In fact, despite the difference in ideology and programs, most of the opposition parties came together to form an anti-congress front in many states of India.

There was another problem embedded within Congress which was worse than the outer problems. The challenge to Indira within the party itself was from the group called "Syndicate", which was led by K. Kamraj, S. K. Patil, N. Sanjeeva Reddy and others. It is interesting that Indira Gandhi owed the position of Prime Minister only because of the support of the syndicate. Now, the same syndicate is on the offensive against Indira Gandhi. After 1967, Indira worked toward regaining ground she lost during the 1967 elections. And for this, she converted a simple power struggle into an ideological struggle. In fact, the Congress Working Committee adopted a Ten Point Program, that included-

1 Social control of banks.
2 Nationalization of General Insurance.
3 Ceiling on urban property and income.
4 Public distribution of food grains.
5 Land reforms and provision of house sites to the rural people.
6 Abolition of the 'privy purse' or the special privileges given to former princes.

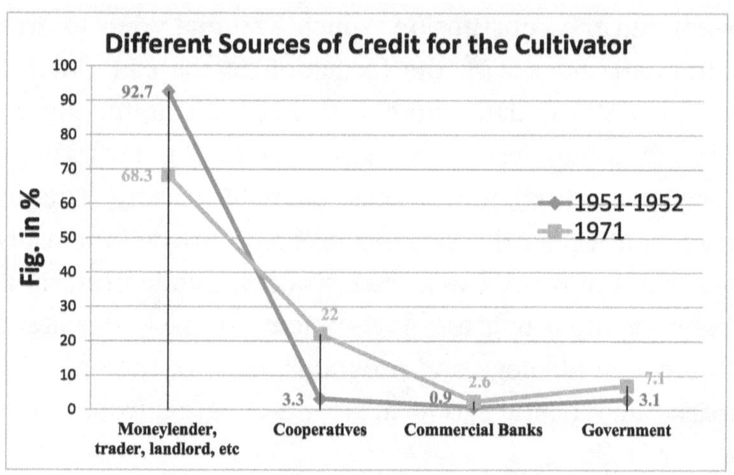

Source: All India Debt and Investment Survey 1961-62,1081. (Cited in Ruddar Dutt, et.al., Indian Economy, pg. 469)

The proclamation of the ten-point program in the CWC was a sinister act for the Syndicate, as they formally approved this to be a left-wing program. Morarji Desai, a leader of the syndicate and the Deputy Prime Minister, openly criticized the policies initiated by CWC and Indira.

However, the challenges to Congress weren't ending there; a new wave of destruction was hung to finally sweep the Congress into two parts. This wasn't far away, a real drama began in 1969, when both the camps within Congress had their own candidates for the post of President of India. This was the last nail in the coffers of Congress when finally, the so-called independent V. V. Giri defeated the formally declared Sanjeeva Reddy of the Congress, and with the defeat of the official Congress candidate, the split in the Congress was written on the walls. The Congress president expelled the Prime Minister, Indira Gandhi, from the party on the ground of disgracing the whip of the party in the

India's Presidential election. In November, 1969, the Congress was split into Congress (O) and Congress (R). Indira projected the split as an ideological divide between socialists and conservatives, where the Syndicate was with "Haves" and Indira proclaimed herself to be with "Haves Not'.

In the general elections held in 1967 and thereafter before 1971, the Congress, besieged by internal dissensions and factionalism, not only lost more than a hundred seats but also saw a decline of four percent in popular votes. The creation of the syndicate undoubtedly has its roots in Nehru's strong leadership that created insecurities and fear among the powerful leaders of the Congress. Though he remained silent all through Nehru's rule, he later found the platform to harm the image of the Congress party. Even many right-wing opportunistic leaders who were waiting for an opportunity to air their ideology, saw in Indira's early rule an appropriate time to take advantage in full swing and bring the hazardous end to Congress and its principles. Eventually, the split within Congress, and thereby the formation of two separate Congresses—Congress (R), popularly known as Indira Congress, and the second, Congress (O), of the Syndicate. By now it was clear that Congress (R) occupied the place more as the left-of-centre position in Indian politics, whereas, the Congress (O) was right-of-centre. Anyhow, in principles, Indira's Congress was ousted from the real Congress, but later in the years and even to this day, the same Congress is known to be the real Congress. The same wasn't thought by many political analysts of the time. In fact, many of them were hoping the end Indira's political career. Did the speculation come true? How Indira and her Congress were able to reestablish the Congress (R), as the major party of all the sections of India.

A New Election and Surprise Restoration of Congress led by Indira – However, the split in the Congress reduced Indira's government to a minority, yet the government continued with the support of parties like CPI and DMK. Indira and the Congress used this period in their vigorous campaign and attempted to project their socialistic credentials. This was done in the hope of strengthening her own party. In 1970, the Congress government surprisingly recommended the dissolution of the Lok Sabha, and with it, India went into elections in the second month of 1971. The recommendation by Indira was astonishing for several analysts who consider Indira's Congress to be just a faction and a weak party. Indeed, the atmosphere sounded like it was uploaded against Congress (R). Nine out of the ten were ready to bet on the Congress (O), as they believed that the real organizational strength lies with the syndicate. Worst was about to thrive for Indira, when non-communist and non-congress opposition parties united together into an alliance. Despite all the verdicts and predictions, Indira and her Congress brought all the major parties on their toes. The Congress (R) and its partner CPI combined won 375 seats in the Lok Sabha and secured 48.4 percent of the votes. Contrary to the success of Indira's Congress, the Congress (O) fell apart with just sixteen Lok Sabha seats and around of the votes, while the Grand Alliance proved to be a grand failure with the tally reaching merely around forty seats, a disappointing show. How was it done? Did Indira have a magical wand to hypnotize the large Indian population?

INC Position in Lok Sabha Elections from 1952 to 1971

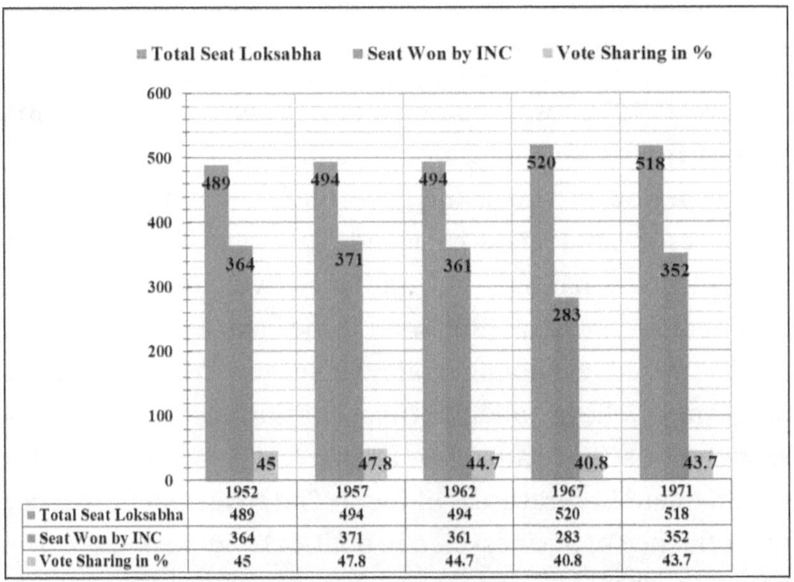

	1952	1957	1962	1967	1971
Total Seat Loksabha	489	494	494	520	518
Seat Won by INC	364	371	361	283	352
Vote Sharing in %	45	47.8	44.7	40.8	43.7

No, no, not at all. In fact, the Congress and Indira only had positive slogans and the work that they continued to do over the years for the people was the only wand that they were equipped with. On the other hand, the opposition or Grand Alliance wasn't equipped with a coherent political program nor had any positive slogan to influence the voters except the "Indira Hatao'. Whereas, the Congress led by Indira Gandhi focused on the growth of the public sector, the imposition of the ceiling act, the removal of disparities in income and opportunity, and the abolition of princely privileges. With the slogan of 'Garibi Hatao', Congress expanded its support base among the landless laborers, Dalits, Adivasis, minorities, women, and unemployed youth. In very different circumstances, Congress came back into power. Soon the second war was forced on India by Pakistan, but Indira and Congress remained agile and gave a fitting reply to Pakistan by ensuring the liberation of Bangladesh. Thus, a new nation emerged in the east after the crushing defeat of Pakistan.

The year 1972, was commemorated as the twenty-fifth year of India's independence, also marked the beginning of a new period in which the government undertook several measures to implement its agenda. In August 1972, general insurance was nationalized, and only five months later, the coal industry. But at the same time, she looked forward to the mixed economic policy. The government-initiated program of cheap foodgrain distribution to the vulnerable sections of society and also launched schemes for creating employment in rural areas of India. The government reduced the influence of businessmen in politics by imposing a ban on donations through joint-stock companies to political parties. It was the time when India achieved a major success in the field of science and technology when the Atomic Energy Commission detonated an underground nuclear device at Pokhran on May 18, 1974.

For the first twenty-five since the enforcement of the Indian Constitution, there had been many ups and downs on various platforms. The early Congress government of Nehru started the journey as an omnibus party which co-opted the ideological shades of the right-center-left and built a consensus to rule India, giving no leeway to political parties of left and right orientation to spread their political and electoral wings. Despite ideological conflict in the party, it was never affected by the transition in India. Nehru, himself, took the initiative for advancing the country. Congress was aware of the value of health and education in creating a strong India. In fact, Nehru once said that a better social order could only be established through proper education. With such a vision, Congress established the pillars of education, science, and technology, and the gazebo of art and culture. Congress didn't stop only with internal development, but initiated policies to have strong tie-ups with foreign countries. The eight-year Panchsheel treaty was signed between China and India in 1954 to respect the territorial integrity and sovereignty of each other. Back home, Congress played a significant role in the unification of the country and promoted unity in diversity. In parliament and within congress internal debates, the congress adopted the policy of coherent, instead of subjugating the opponent. This enhanced the country's march toward a strong democracy. Though at the same time, the ruling congress faced new challenges in building the nation and there were limitations also, but the willpower and determination of the leaders from Nehru, Shastri, and Indira made it easy for the congress to cross over the flooded river of crisis. Through the first twenty-five years of Congress rule, mainly on planning, which strove to transform India from a traditional to a modern society and towards a welfare state, as the plight of the people of then was miserable.

The decade of the seventies brought significant change in the politics of India. The Congress had now lost its ground, though it had taken upheaval task to march on the mixed economy despite the opposition from opposition parties as well as inside Congress. The bottom line is that, throughout the 50s, 60s, and first five years of 70s, Congress remained the party that was more compelled to work for the cause of building a strong India in terms of political, social, culture and economy. Being a ruling party for all these years, despite of challenges, the Congress played a major role in the nation building in India. Some of the major ingredient that advanced the country towards a new horizon are as follows-

- Well-articulated and well-functioning constitution, the backbone of Indian democracy.
- Capacity to bring peaceful and constitutional means of political change.
- Unity in Diversity.
- Communication and Infrastructure.
- Development of Economy.
- Safeguarding the minorities and weaker sections of the society.
- Achievement of National goals and objectives.

04

An Era of Success and Downfall: 1975 to 2000

The Time Line of Congress (1975-2000)

1975	• Imposition of Emergency
1977	• Massive defeat in General Election for Congress and Victory of Janata Party
1978	• Split in Congress • Congress swipes the state election of Andhra and Karnataka under the leadership of Indira Gandhi
1980	• Massive victory in the Lok Sabha election for Congress (Secured more than 300 seats)
1984	• Indira Gandhi was assassinated on Oct 31, 1984
1984-1989	**• Main Contribution** • Mizo-Assam-Punjab Accord • First step to change political and economic climate • Lost the majority, but remained the largest Party.
1989	• Lost the majority, but remained the largest party
1991	• Rajiv Gandhi's assassination • Non-Gandhian and Nehruvian prime minister, P.V. Narasimha Rao. • Step towards opening up the economy for global Market
1996	• Congress lost general Election.
1998	• Sonia Gandhi becomes the President of Congress • Towards the Road of Recovery by winning the state election in Madhya Pradesh, Rajasthan and Delhi
1999	• More wins for Congress in States- Goa, Maharashtra and Arunachal Pradesh
2000	• Back to back victories in the states like Assam, Kerala and Pondicherry

The last twenty-five years of the 20th century can be recalled for different kinds of turmoil for Congress as well as for overall Indian politics. India's two Prime Ministers, Indira Gandhi and Rajeev Gandhi, were both assassinated. Unfortunately, he couldn't serve the country for long, except for one tenure, i.e., from 1984 to 1989. He was then ousted from power and finally lost his life in a human bomb attack in Tamil Naidu. We shall talk about his contribution and also his drawbacks later in this chapter. Despite a significant decline in the party's consolidation or perhaps as a result of some hasty decisions, whatever the issue, their contribution to the Congress party and to Indian politics cannot be denied or underestimated. Despite the difference in approach, both were the stalwart leaders of the Congress; their success was approved in the successive win of Congress in the electoral politics. Although there was a time when Congress was invaded by opposition and turncoat leaders, this was only for a short period of time as it evolved from failure to immiscible success politically, socially, and ideologically. But as every coin has two faces, so does Congress. It went through various phases in the last twenty-five years of the 20th century. Indeed, Congress itself tainted some of its old values and ideologies. For a while, it appeared that Nehruvian ideas were those of an old monk. Secularism lost its radiance when the Congress (directly or indirectly) promoted the heinous and ferocious act of massacring Sikhs following Mrs. Indira Gandhi's assassination by a Sikh bodyguard; it was claimed that the act was retaliation for the "Blue Operation." The Congress was in power at the centre, but did nothing to address the BJP's open crime, then to connivance. It appeared as though; Congress was complicit in the crime. The last two and a half decades of the twentieth century were abysmal for the Congress; it not only faced crushing defeat after the internal Emergency in 1977, but it was also deposed from power in 1989, 1996, and 1998. The Gandhian shadow remained murky in the Congress during the 1990s. This could be one of the reasons for the subsequent decline in the popular support of the Congress and also the uprising of right-wing upheaval in the political horizon of India.

The story of Congress advances in tandem with India's political ups and downs. The few decades following independence were unquestionably surpassed in the glories of Congress, when it garnered from the legacy of the national movement, and Nehru remained the undisputed leader for the right-centre-left wings of the political shadows. The legacy of Nehru was and remained alive even in the decades of the 60s and 70s, though it has been observed that descendent voices against the Congress were making their own route; these emerged both ways, i.e., within the grand old party as well as in other parties and their volatile leaders. In fact, it was the time when the Congress was on the verge of losing its own ground among the Indian masses for a variety of known and unknown reasons. One reason, among others, was Mrs. Indira Gandhi's led Congress's abrupt nationalisation of banks, insurance, and other industries, which elicited a harsh reaction from right-wing leaders within and outside the Congress. While some political analysts dismiss such flawed arguments, instead alleges that dynastic succession was the real cause of inner-party conflict in the Congress. Whatever the reason, regardless of the postulated propaganda and split, Indira's Congress not only won the Lok Sabha election of 1971, but also made history by securing 352 Lok Sabha seats and a four percent increase in vote share. It was unprecedented. Especially, after the split in Congress and the manner in which all eminent leaders shifted their loyalty in 1969, only few political analysts predicted about such a miracle to occur in favour of Congress and Mrs. Indira. However, Indira proved herself to be the undisputed leader of the Congress through her miraculous efforts and the charismatic political vision. Her charismatic personality not only brought defeat for the opponents, but they had to bite the dust. Because of the overwhelming support that she received; she was given free rein to pursue nationalisation. According to reports, the main reasons for nationalisation were to protect jobs and to protect the interests of organised labour.

People always think that history proceeds in a straight line. It doesn't. Social attitudes don't change in a straight line. There is always a backlash against progressive ideas. So, politics also doesn't move in a straight line; there are always twist and turn. Very soon, it will be realised that the situation would be grim for both the Congress and Mrs. Indira Gandhi.

The Pre-Emergency Crisis – In 1975, India experienced its greatest ever crisis, and to combat it, the Indira Gandhi-led Congress government had no other alternative than to declare an Internal Emergency. How did the Emergency come about? Was it the nostalgia of Indira? Or was something baking behind the wall, which was read by the Congress? Whatever be but, it is quite agreeable that the situation was complex.

Indeed, it was the time when India was experiencing many ups and downs. A large-scale frustration among the youths was shaping because of unemployment and economic recession, the natural calamity like irregular monsoon had added wound to the pathetic condition of farmers and working class in the Indian society due the severe rise in the price of food grains, and other essential commodities. Another factor that overshadowed the Congressmen's judgement was internal conflict. At last, but still most importantly, the opponents were clustering together as a larger united force to capitalise on the furore and rage of the people, particularly the youth. All this made the situation unmanageable for Congress. It is said that the unrest was so desperate that thousands of students came out on the streets of the towns and cities, first in Gujarat and later in Bihar which was very soon supported by the opposition parties. In fact, the Bihar movement led by Jay Prakash Narayana (JP) was dubbed "Waterloo". It was a tug of war, and Indira's refusal to concede the demands for the dissolution of the assembly aggravated matters, and the smoke that had erupted in Bihar had now spread to the rest of the country. It was a tug of war, and Indira's refusal to concede the demands for the dissolution of the assembly aggravated matters, and the smoke that had erupted in Bihar had now spread to the rest of the country. All of the major non-left political parties supported it. Soon the movement faded. However, a new controversy that fueled the opposition led by JP was the Allahabad High Court Verdict, which stated that Mrs. Gandhi could not contest election for parliament or hold the Prime Minister's office for six years. Another was the jolt in the Gujarat Assembly election result for the congress was yet another political setback. Both of these events rekindled the opposition movement and on corruption charges demanded resignation of Mrs. Gandhi. Once again, in a vast scale the protest began which took various forms to bring an end to the Indira regime. Finally, in response to the upheaval, Indira and Congress declared an internal emergency on June 26, 1975.

Both the camps made their justification to justify their means, but certainly, it was the first time in the history of post-independent India that democracy came under the scrutiny. Taking this into consideration, the acts of Indira led Congress and JP led opposition nevertheless, shunned all possibilities of elections, which for sure are wheels of democracy.

Almost two years of disappointment and hopes – Article 352 of the constitution declared a state of internal emergency, which halted all normal political processes. It suspended the federal provisions of the constitution and the fundamental rights of the people. The government imposed strict censorship on the press, and hundreds of the main opposition leaders were arrested under the MISA. Several extreme communal and ultra-left organizations were banned. It is estimated that approximately one lakh people were arrested from all over the country. Those arrested included the leaders of the opposition parties, anti-social elements like smugglers, hoarders, black marketeers, etc. Things ended there, but a series of decrees, laws, and constitutional amendments reduced the judiciary's powers to check the executive's functioning. It was an open attack on the check and balance system, which is the foundation of democracy. But contrary to popular belief, the emergency also brought hope for many. It was the Twenty Point Program which was implemented seriously for the upliftment of the socio-economic platform for the vast section of the rural poor. In the beginning, it looked as if the people accepted the emergency, but soon became disillusioned and surrounded, and as a result, popular discontent reached its maximum because of the increased power of unchecked bureaucracy and the police. Amidst various shades of emergency, suddenly, on January 18, 1977, Indira announced the end of the emergency and called for the Lok Sabha election. This election has been a testing ground for Indian democracy, and undoubtedly it has proven and revealed the people's attachment to democratic values. The free and fair election also marks the great faith of Congress and Mrs. Gandhi in democratic values, despite the fact, there have been several allegations against Congress and Mrs. Gandhi for their anti-democratic role during the time of emergency. The Congress saw a catastrophic wipe out in the 1977 election. Even Mrs. Gandhi herself couldn't save her seat. Despite the severe defeat, the Congress Party won 154 Lok Sabha seats and remained an opposition party in the Lok Sabha. Unlike the family of different ideologies and faith, the Janata Party overwhelmingly won the Lok Sabha, but despite the well-defined majority, it couldn't complete the five-year tenure because of the inner conflict for the highest post. Finally, in 1979, the Janata Party rule collapsed, and it had a dramatic end. Because Morarji couldn't hold his Prime Minister post for a long time because of infighting among the leaders for the lust of seeking the highest post, a new election was called to take place at the beginning of the next year, i.e., in January 1980.

Meanwhile, Congress faced yet another split in 1978, and Indira and her supporters eventually decided to secede from the old party, Congress (R), and formed a new opposition party, Congress (I), with "I" standing for Indira. Only in 1996 was the "I" designation dropped. However, a landslide victory for the newly formed Congress (I) once again proved the efficiency of Mrs. Gandhi's efficiency as a stateswoman.

Nevertheless, the decades of the 70s and early 80s will also be remembered in the history of Congress and its electoral failure. Indeed, Congress has failed to pass the litmus test of electoral politics on several occasions. Over the years, there have been mixed responses to Congress' electoral politics, as its popularity has never been consistent.

Internal disturbance and Assassination of Mrs. Gandhi – The new party proven a panacea once again to Congress and Mrs. Gandhi, a landslide victory brought the other parties on dearth. 353 Lok Sabha seats and the vote share of almost forty-three percent was a remarkable performance from any point of view. But very soon, the Congress government in the centre faced the problems in Assam, Punjab and Kashmir. The issues were intractable and arose out of the Communal, linguistic and caste conflicts. The other big issue was the atrocity against the Scheduled Caste and tribes who asserted their social and constitutional rights. However, amidst all these problems, Congress continued to walk on the road of economic development. It was the time when the world economy was changing rapidly, and India wasn't left of the mounting pressure of the changing world market where MNCs and Private sectors were ready to erode in the self-reliance India. In such a grim situation strengthening the public sector was a courageous job that the Congress successfully was able to continue. In fact, the Congress government successfully raised the economy growth, and also brought down the rate of inflation rate seven percent in 1984.

It was also the period when the Congress government attempted to improve India's relations with the United States while also attempting to normalise relations with both of India's neighbours, China and Pakistan. However, the internal situation remained precarious due to Jarnail Singh Bhindranwale and his militant followers' rise and later intensification of conflict in Punjab for Sikh autonomy. Bhindranwale is said to have stationed himself in the Golden Temple in Amritsar with his militant supporters. Congress's union government attempted to negotiate on several occasions but was unsuccessful. Seeing no success through the talks and realising that any lapse would have grave consequences for the security of the country, the Congress government finally ordered the Indian Army to enter the Golden Temple in June 1984 to end the rising menace.

The successful eviction of the Golden Temple from the clutches of Bhindranwale and his followers was the result of Operation Blue Star, but this act induced unrest among a section of the Sikh community, eventually which led to the act of cowardice by her own bodyguards on October 31, 1984. It was the day when Mrs. Gandhi was shot dead in the name of religion despite the fact that she was a staunch secularist in principles and practices.

The assassination of Mrs. Gandhi brought the country on the halt for a moment, and then the bloody tragedy began on the roads of the country, especially north and North-western part of the country. The country's capital city was flooded with massacres of innocent Sikhs. Their homes and shops were ransacked, and women were raped by unknown miscreants (some claim that the RSS was responsible for 'teaching' the Sikh community a lesson, while others claim that Congressmen engaged in barbaric retaliation). Whatever the truth is, the heinous act killed thousands of Sikh community members and caused thousands more to lose their homes and businesses. The roads had become macabre for a few days and had haunted the Sikhs for many years.

Amid the heinous crime committed on the capital city's roads, lanes and colonies, and it appeared that the miscreant was given free-hand was given for some time to teach 'lesson', the prince was crowned to replace the assassinated head. Don't you think this one act of Congress has blurred its image of secularism?

Soft Hinduism or Secularism – There has been dispute among political analysts regarding the rise of Hinduism or Hindu Chauvinistic ideology. Some believe that its growth perpetuated after the arrival of coalition Janata Dal government, whereas other believe that the rise of Hinduism had started taking shape in Congress rule itself. At least, Congress's landslide victory in the election of 1984 confirms and points toward this argument more than any other. This was the election that was contested directly on the ground of sympathy for Rajeev Gandhi, who lost his mother when she was assassinated because, for her, the utmost priority was the nation. Indeed, it was the first occasion, when Congress seemed like camouflage. However, the emotional appeal brought a landslide victory for Congress. It won 415 Lok Sabha seats, the most in India's independent history, and received more than 49 percent of the vote.

After the death of Mrs. Gandhi, the new and much more reluctant Prime Minister, Mr. Rajeev Gandhi, despite the travails, took off on a positive note. At the political level, the Congress Ministry set in motion the process for the Punjab and Assam accords. On August 15, 1985, the Assam Accord was signed in the presence of Prime Minister Rajiv Gandhi and Prafulla Mahanta, Bhrigu Kumar Phukan, and Biraj Sharma, the leaders of the Assam agitation, signed a Memorandum of Settlement (MoS) to bring an end to the Assam agitation, while the Rajiv-Longo Wal Accord was signed on July 24, 1985, between the Government of India and the Akali Dal, to bring an end to the agitation. Another accord that was signed by Prime Minister Rajiv Gandhi and Sri Lankan President J. R. Jayewardene to resolve the ongoing problem of civil war between the Sri Lankan government and the LTTE, a Tamil rebel group, but this accord backfired when the LTTE refused to disarm, and later in the years, this group assassinated Rajiv Gandhi to take revenge in retaliation.

Other than the issues of the political sphere, Congress also unveiled the New National Policy on Education, which emphasised the removal of disparities and equalising educational opportunities for women, SCs, and STs. The policy later emphasised on the opening of the Open University System and improving the primary schooling system.

The Congress, under the leadership of Rajiv Gandhi, also brought in the telecom revolution by setting up the MTNL in 1986. This was also the time when a big push was given to India's computerization program, though it had already been formulated by Mrs. Indira Gandhi. This was also the time when lucrative policies were taken to enhance domestic production and also allow foreign manufacturers to try their fate in the Indian market. The Congress, as the ruling party, went ahead with the modernization of the armed forces by doubling the defence expenditure and purchasing several modern and well-sophisticated weapons. But who knew then that his own policies would be a boomerang for the Congress and Rajiv Gandhi? The corruption charges in the Bofors deal emerged ruthlessly from the bowl, not only haunting but also agonising Congress over and over.

The period between 1985 and 1989 witnessed a gradual shift in Congress's policies from the legacy of the past. Indeed, it enhanced the concept of the welfare state, and that is why, despite the tilt in the policy, it introduced the Mahatma Gandhi National Rural Employment Guarantee Act (MGNREGA) with the objective of "enhancing livelihood security in rural areas by providing a hundred days of guaranteed wage employment in a financial year to every household."

Anyhow, this period would also be remembered for the pro-Hindu and protector of the minority's stance of Congress. Earlier by remaining silent, Congress gave green signal to the mob attack on Sikhs in 1984, and once again allowing Shilanyas (laying Foundation ceremony) adjacent to the disputed site of Ram Janmabhoomi proved its soft stand toward Hindu fundamentalists. Another story that faced heavy criticism was the nullification of the Supreme Court's judgement in the Shah Bano Case. The pro-Hindu and anti-women stance of the Congress turned a wider section of progressives away from the Congress and they started looking for new opportunities. This section saw V. P. Singh's Janata Dal with optimism.

It was also the period when the Congress government walked away from its principle of mixed economy and fostering the socialistic approach. Instead, it now capitalised and bent itself toward privatisation, liberalisation, and globalisation policies, and planned to cede the market to the world market, though reluctantly and secretly. It was also the time that on several occasions, at least two times, the Congress looked to be leaving the path of secularism, which heavily cost not only Congress, but the nation had to bear the cost of, and is still paying for it. The culture of corruption spread in each branch from the top to the bottom of the system, which slaughtered the moral and ethical values of the leaders as well as ordinary Indians. Overall, the beginning was on a positive note, but steadily the Congress situation wobbled.

The 1989 general election proved a disaster for Congress. The Janata Dal, led by V. P. Singh, pulled the crowd into the booth to vote against corruption and for the implementation of the recommendation of the Mandal Commission; which had been in abeyance for a long time after being tabled once. Now the djinn was once again out. The Grand Alliance took advantage of the Congress' fraying nerves and, secondly, targeted OBCs and other backward classes to a large extent to further damage the Congress. There was a dip of almost ten percent in votes for Congress and a loss of 218 seats. Nevertheless, Congress and Rajiv Gandhi succeeded in placing the idea of preparing for the 21st century in the minds of thinking Indians. In any case, V. P. Singh was instrumental in uniting the Communists and the right-wing BJP on opposing sides. He placated the left or Communist parties by calling them his natural allies, but also ensured to keep the BJP under his arm by speaking from their platform. We shall sometime later discuss how this strategy of both the Left parties and V. P. Singh, later in the years, proved to be catastrophic not only for the two political parties, but now it is challenging the whole social structure and Constitution of India.

In the shadow of the left and right parties, they formed the government at the end of 1989 and could hold office for merely a period of a year and a half year. The small duration would be remembered for the two main objectives.

1 Implementation of Mandal Commission Report and thereafter a massive outrage of the upper caste youths and the student, indulging in violence and self-immolation, and from the government part massive crackdown to bring an end to the ongoing rage.
2 Meanwhile, Bhartiya Janata Party (BJP) got the opportunity to go ahead with its own agenda of Ram Janam Bhoomi. The prominent leader of then, Mr. L. K. Advani started the 'Rath Yatra' from Somnath (Gujarat) to Ayodhya, which ended with the arrest of L. K. Advani in Bihar and withdrawing the support from the existing Union government of Janata Dal.

But by now the situation had become alarming, and the growth of BJP was a precedent very soon. Definitely, what Jan Sangh couldn't succeed in doing between 1977-1979, BJP was able to exploit the opportunity to surface its agendas among a vast section of the Hindu mindset.

Last Decade of the Millennium and the beginning of Pro-Hindu Stance – Finally, after a year and a half of rule, the Janata Dal rule came to an end, and the declaration for the eleventh Lok Sabha Election was officially announced by the Election Commission of India. The first phase was over and Rajiv Gandhi was campaigning for the next round of elections. Unfortunately, one night when Rajiv had to address the crowd close to Chennai, he was blown to pieces by a young woman. It is said she was an LTTE militant who was looking for revenge against Rajiv Gandhi for the Sri Lanka Accord, which they thought was against the LTTE movement and favoured the Sri Lankan government. It was a shock to the country and to Congress itself. But in the political arena, the act of cowardice generated a sympathy wave in favour of Congress, giving them the tally of 232 seats and the status of the single largest party. Though it was short of the absolute majority for the Congress, it was enough to form the minority government of Narasimha Rao. Later, his government was able to successfully garner the majority. It was twenty-five years since Congress was going to rule the country in the absence of dynastic succession.

The absence meant a lot in the accumulation of new policies and making shifts from the old position. Since the implementation of the Constitution of India and the establishment of India as a republic in the early years of the last decade of the twentieth century, India has been inspired by Gandhian and Nehruvian thoughts. A little shift in the policies was taking place now and then, but this was only the beginning. The arrival of Narasimha Rao, a face other than the family of Gandhi, brought a radical change in the economic structure as well as the Congress stance on the question of secularism seemed to be trembling from its old and official stand. He embarked upon dismantling the license. Raj, though he faced a stiff challenge within the party, as a section of the party leaders, took this action against the very ideology of the Congress. However, in some ways, such changes were the need of the hour to avert the impending 1991 economic crisis. He laid the red carpet for foreign investment, and to resolve the purpose, he headed toward reforming capital markets, deregulation of domestic business, and also significant change in the trade regime. The primary goals of these reforms were to reduce the fiscal deficit, privatise the public sector, and increase infrastructure investment. It was during Narasimha Rao's premiership, India subsequently headed to further develop its extensive economic and strategic relationship with the nations of Southeast Asia to bolster its standing as a regional power and to counterbalance the strategic influence of China. The Prime Minister, Narasimha Rao's office, was known for distancing itself from Nehruvian socialism and paving the way for the policies dictated by the IMF and World Bank. Secondly, the demolition of Babri Masjid tarnished its long-developed image of a secular party. The Muslim, progressive, and secular sections of Indian society were disheartened by such a move, and in later years, Congress couldn't find an abyss for its grieves and sorrows and was still searching for a recovery with little hope. In a nutshell, the five years of Narasimha Rao gave the BJP the opportunity for political space, which resulted in the loss of Congress and marked the beginning of a new era, which, while still in its infancy, undoubtedly marked a bright future for the saffron ideology and party. The Congress citadel was on the verge of decline. Finally, it was in the year 1999, the BJP became the single largest party by winning 182 seats and formed a coalition government by forming the National Democratic Alliance (NDA) at the Centre under the leadership of Atal Behari Vajpayee.

By this time, the Congress had realised that the BJP was poised to exploit the Congress's weaknesses. Seeing no other option, Sonia Gandhi, the wife of Mr. Rajiv Gandhi, who had stayed out of politics until then, was invited to serve as the Congress's president in the hope of defeating the BJP. Her entry into Congress was agile and contributed to the awakening of the hibernating rank and files of the party. Very soon the BJP could smell the heat when Congress was able to clinch victories one after the other from 1998 to 2004. The years 1998, 1999, 2000, 2001, and 2003 were witnessed as a massive sweep in several states, and finally, 2004 proved a nightmare for the saffron party when Congress hilariously formed Dr. Manmohan Singh's government in the Centre, despite the loud claims of the BJP and against all predictions of political pundits. Sonia's arrival can be marked as the third phase of Congress, which arrested the imminent decline and also brought Congress back to power at the Centre in 2004. However, the BJP's victory must be sustained in the twenty-first century, or the Congress will fall to the bottom. We shall discuss this in the next chapter.

Anyway, the last twenty-five years have been filled with many ups and downs on the political stage for Congress. On several occasions, it seemed that Congress wouldn't stand anywhere or would be at the bottom of the political sphere, but every time it was proven wrong to everyone. This period also witnessed crushing defeats for Congress on several occasions. It also witnessed the tragic loss of its two leaders, who were assassinated but hailed as martyrs for their unexceptional courage in fighting for the right cause, but at the same time, some drastic move called the party's ideology and policies into question, as it departed from its previous stance on socialism and secularism. It has also been noticed that whenever

Congress found itself trapped in any crisis, it was the Nehru-Gandhi family that brought the party out of critical situations; the story from Indira Gandhi to Sonia Gandhi has the same narrative.

The 1990s observed the decaying of the Nehruvian ideas of modern India, which was carried by the Congress since 1947 onward, and continued even in its worst political situation. Now the same ideology had become trivial and rhetoric for the Congressmen. The Nehruvian idea of mixed economy was now sung rhetorically to appease the audience, but in real world the Congress had made up its mind to devoid with it, and march toward capitalism monopoly. In other words, Congress in the leadership of Narasimha Rao and his finance Minister Dr. Manmohan Singh over-shadowed the traditional Congress theory of mixed economy idea and the welfare Indian state. Now, there was commotion for liberalization, globalization and privatization. They prophesied about the new economy policy. Furthermore, the dent came to one of the pillars of constitution i.e., "Socialism", when Atal Bihari Vajpayee, the right-wing leader of Bhartiya Janata Party formed the government in 1998 and later in 1999 with the support of scores of other parties, called the National Democratic Alliance. Earlier, the same party vigorously called for "Swadeshi", but in 1999, as soon as, they formed the government, became raincoat of their own words. Apparently, this was the time when the new economy policies of Narasimha-Manmohan kicked the deck nakedly. Obviously, the right-wing Bhartiya Janata Party always been fore runner against the mixed economy, and often criticized the Nehruvian policies as pro – Soviet.

Finally, the Congress remained a party of various colours in the last twenty-five years, though subsequently, the drift in the ideology and policies was foreseen, but was the shift temporary or permanent? We shall try to search for it in the new millennium that was at the corner.

05

Inclusion of Capitalism and Syncretism: A New Style of Congress

The last decade of the millennium was horrifying for the Congress, though it formed the government in 1991, but the party was tremendously worried and immensely pressurized with sinking popularity of the party and the downcast of ideology. Already, Narasimha Rao and Dr. Manmohan Singh had crippled the old wagon of exemplary mixed economy, which was tributed to them by Jawaharlal Nehru, and nourished by Mrs. Indira Gandhi. While on social status, the Congress faced a nightmare on the issue of secularism which had been the legacy of the Congress, not only in the post-independent India, but in fact strongly the culture of unity dominated in the pre-independence era also. The weakness in the organization, the inner-party conflict, allegations of corruption, shunning of minorities, especially Muslims cost dearly to the party in the elections in the years 1996, 1998 and 1999. In fact, in the 1999 elections, Congress declined to an incredible 114 seats, the lowest ever in the history of electoral politics. It was a dismal performance for Congress, while Bhartiya Janata Party able to muster the support of as much as thirteen other parties under the leadership of Mr. Atal Behari Vajpayee sailed to form the government first in 1998 and later in 1999. Though, earlier in 1996, it was able to garner the support, as a result Atal Behari Vajpayee could sustain only for a few days.

Amidst of the severe blow, the Congress leader urged Mrs. Sonia Gandhi (who repelled herself from any sought political activities) to the responsibility of consolidating the hibernating Congress. Her efforts bore fruit soon in consecutive wins in the various states' assembly, but soon some Congress leaders detached from the Congress because of her Italian ethnicity. Indeed, in the early years, all wasn't well, she struggled to revive the party. In the leadership of Mrs. Sonia Gandhi, the party finally took the decision to abandon the policy of 'Ekla Chalo', and formed alliances with other like-minded parties, and soon the party found itself ruling as much as in fifteen states. With this possible success, Congress geared up for the 2004 general elections.

A new millennium brought a new hope for Congress after being almost rampaged in the last decade of the twentieth century. The dawn of the millennium and a new century brought a new hope to Congress. The dream was successfully met in 2004 general election when United Progressive Alliance (UPA) in the leadership of Mrs. Sonia Gandhi touched the number of 244, though still was away from the majority, but abled to garnered the support of smaller parties to form the government with Dr. Manmohan Singh as Prime Minister. The success of Congress came because of the two broader reasons – first was the performance of National Democratic Alliance, definitely on the issue of economy the things were under the control of Vajpayee's government, but on other platforms like internal and external security the government on at least a couple of occasions; Kargil war and the Kandahar incident brought the shame for the government, corruption charges also tarnished the reputation of the government; the Unit Trust of India scam, in which small investors lost their savings, allotment of more three thousands petrol pumps, gas agencies and kerosene dealerships to BJP and RSS leaders and their relatives by the Petroleum Minister, Rama Naik created commotion in the parliament for several days.

Internally, the Vishwa Hindu Parishad, Bajrang Dal and RSS were not ready to tame themselves, but, on the contrary, had every intention to use state power to fulfil their long-cherished dream to create a Hindu Rashtra, eventually laid the foundation for the communal tension in all over the country, and finally Gujarat became the epic-centre for the horrible act of genocide of minority, Muslims. The education wasn't spared, it was targeted with conspiracy to communalize the education. All these, and many more fumed the ordinary masses.

On the other hand, Congress utilized the opportunity at its best to consolidate its workers and voters. In fact, the state assembly election had filled the Congressmen with zeal and enthusiasm. Congress had already set up its agenda for the campaign, it targeted and emphasized on social inclusion and welfare of the common masses. The Congress used the attractive slogan to please the common masses like, "Congress ka haath, Aam aadmi ke saath" against the glittering but not effective by any means of "India Shining". Hence, by virtue of the effective campaign and drawbacks of the NDA government, United Progressive Alliance (UPA), led by Congress managed substantial lead on NDA by bagging overall 222 seats, but not enough for majority. Finally, the Communist front led by CPM made its entry for the rescue operational work. The entry and supporting Dr. Manmohan led UPA government by Communist front was an interesting part, as earlier, it has been volatile against the implementation of New Economy Policy of Narasimha and Dr. Manmohan. And now, the architect of the reforms was set to become the Prime Minister. Was it sarcastic or ironic, that we will discuss in the later stage of the chapter.

Dr. Manmohan, the Prime Miniter and the advent of New Model – As the new autumn arrives with shooting of buds and then spread its fragrance on every one and to all parts without any discrimination and biasness, so was followed by the newly elected government of UPA whose string was in the hands of the two different ideological pillars; Mrs. Sonia Gandhi and the Communist Front led by CPM. Thus, it was triangular contest – Mrs. Sonia Gandhi had the legacy of her mother-in-law and husband of Nehru thought, CPM, a disciplined party of cadres stood firmly on the Marxist philosophy of working class, whereas, Dr. Manmohan wanted to started all over again to take India on the horizon of new economy; an economy of privatization, liberalization and globalization, in short transfer of economy from the social perspective to centralized economy in the private hands. This model, he had earlier initiated and to some extent implemented as the finance minister during the Congress rule 1991-1996. But this time the situation was a little different than earlier one. The Congress had witnessed the drastic decline after the advent of the New Economic Policy. The Hindu newspaper expressed the views of many while describing the verdict against the NDA, 'it was clear outrage against the NDA's policies', further India Shining campaign was blown apart even before the start. Atal Behari Vajpayee rode on the chariot of Swadeshi to come into power, but soon carried the pro-capitalism policies to lay the red carpet for the MNCs and for Indian industrialist tycoons. Earlier, the Narasimha's Government also failed to take advantage of the reforms initiated by his government; it boomeranged both the times in the defeat firstly to Congress and later the NDA led by Atal Behari Vajpayee met with the same fate. In a nutshell, the new government because of the previous experiences and secondly due to immense pressure of the left front forwarded a new theory-reforms with human face. In fact, to assist the government in policy formulation a National Advisory Council was set up, with representatives of civil society, intellectuals and experts as its members, and Sonia Gandhi at its head. Within the Congress the leadership was diluted from a single person to the Manmohan-Sonia-Rahul troika which worked well for five years (2004-2009).

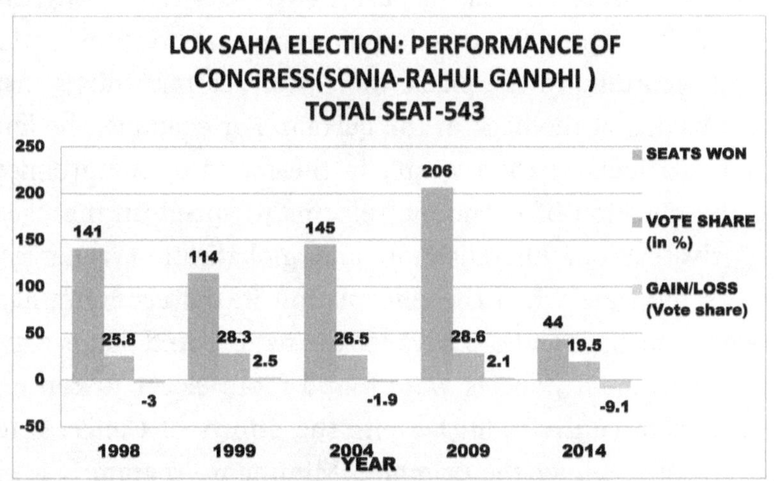

Source: Election Commission of India

The UPA government despite the risk of losing its majority was sailing on the two boats at a time. Stood with trusted faith on toward the economic reforms, and at the same time brought some progressive measures of a welfare state. Though, the UPA was looking ahead to provide all possible platforms to welcome the MNCs by ensuring flexible policies, yet established a syncretic approach. Indeed, the tenure of 2004-2009 of the UPA government will be remembered for its impressive performance, and this made them retain power for the second time in 2009. In fact, Congress increased its seats from a tally of 145 in 2004 to 206, gaining 61 seats, and overall UPA reached 262 seats. The Congress nurtured an impressive performance mainly due to the combined efforts of the tri leadership i.e., Dr. Manmohan-Sonia-Rahul. There were other major issues like the National Rural Employment Guarantee Scheme (NREGS), farm loan waiver scheme, pro-poor policies of the government, confidence of stability and victory over the fundamentalist forces by the secular forces that played sublime role in pushing the UPA and Congress toward the victory. But this doesn't mean that everything was going according to the plans, there were certain things that were baking at the back of the curtain. For example, the left front, particularly CPM wasn't in the mood to compromise on the question of economic reforms to speed up the pace of privatization, liberalization and globalization, whereas, it was the time when the reformation in the economy had become the hard truth to advance the nation. And that is why, the government policies were found more closer to centre-left than to centre-right. Despite the efforts of Congress to compromise as per the Common Minimum Program (CMP) of UPA coalition, some rough obscenity advanced within UPA, especially in 2008, the UPA government found in mess when left front withdrew their support in protest against the India-United States Civil Nuclear Agreement, though it survived the vote of confidence, which was brought on by the left front itself. The things didn't limit to left front criticism of the government, but the coalition party DMK also ruffled around to "declare that genocide and war crimes had been committed on the Eelam Tamils by the Sri Lankan Army and the administrators".

Back to the economy, as many hold the view that UPA's 2004-2014 in terms of economic growth was a lost decade, but they either forget to analyze the ten years of the narrative of the two terms of UPA or they pretend to show things in other ways. Whatever may be the reason, but such views reflect the disarray and aloofness without the subjectivity of the views. As earlier it has been already discussed that despite the compulsion of a minority government, Dr. Manmohan government was able to make inclusion of two different roads of ideology; an ideology of socialism that takes the nation on the path of welfare state, whereas, capitalist thought shrinks the resource into few hands. The UPA government needed to think between the two poles, and that could only be possible by inclusion of both; and in fact, though silently, but able to harness the route between the two. It was syncretism. Undoubtedly, the Prime Minister Mr. Manmohan managed it very well. But the general impression that went around, that UPA has landed the country in an economic mess. There are two instances that reveal how the same narratives were imbibed differently.

- The Congress squandered resources on the folly schemes like NREGA and National Food Security Act, thus reversing liberalization and slowing the pace of sectors like infrastructure. It was well planned propaganda that the right-wing were taking among the masses. On the other hand, the left oriented organizations charged the government for being under massive influence of corporations and against inclusive growth.

But the reality was far away than what was propagated by the two different ideological poles. Dr, Manmohan government compared to the previous rule of NDA was enhancing favorable outcomes on both the platforms, for which the UPA government was being criticized about. If one goes into nuances would find a very different story, then the two tales of opponent camps. Frankly speaking, it was the period when growth accelerated, Indians started making more savings as well as investing, the period also witnessed the opening of the economy, the foreign direct investment rushed in, at the social level poverty reduced further and construction of infrastructure gathered pace. Besides, the capitalist framework, the UPA government also initiated work on the welfare like-several measures, like special concern was given toward nutrition, education, and life expectancy and so on by the government for human development and to effectively implement such needed programs at the grassroot level, the government brought wider sections of scheme like Right to Education, Right to Information. But what was highlighted was very different, the headline glittered with Land Acquisition, but wiped out the cause of grabbing land for the extensive industrialization and infrastructural construction usage. Without any doubt, the period of 2004-2009 could expressed as the golden age of the new millennium, despite the hurdles put in especially by the Left Front, but Dr. Manmohan Singh continued to play the ball on both sides that is advocated and implemented the new economic policy and also constructively brought welfare schemes to keep the balance in the social and political order of India. But sometimes growth even takes the shape of frustrations, precisely because of a rapidly changing economy, and the political parties that use the emotions reap the benefits.

In 2009, though the opponent camps tried to utilize in their own way, but was in vain. As UPA did not form the government for a second consecutive tenure, their seat tally also increased, and more importantly Congress was able to take its tally to 206; a rise of 61 seats. It was unexpected by the political pundits, but the vast Indian masses thought the other way. Thus, one can say that UPA-1 won the initial battle despite the unholy and unrestrained campaign from the counter parts. The tenure of UPA 1 for Congress brought unexpected success by mingling the economic reforms with welfare schemes which was appreciated by a wider section of Indians. It was the time when the UPA government passed several social reform bills for benefitting the underprivileged section of the society, that included – Employment Guarantee bill, Right to Information Act (RTI), the Protection of women from Domestic Violence Act, 2005, and Right to Education (RTE). The UPA government also supported and increased the budget to improve literacy and health care. It is said that the Left Front was the driving force behind to endorse such legislation. Other than the social affairs bill, the UPA government also introduced value-added tax (VAT) to strengthen the economic reforms, also implemented the Goods and Services Tax (GST) during his first tenure. Under the disciplined guidance of the UPA government, India was able to resist the worst affected period of the global economic crisis of 2008. Several pro-people policies and launching various economic reforms worked as the catalyst for the Congress and overall UPA success in 2009 general election, and further the perceived divisiveness policies of the BJP added more to the success. The tenure for the Congress led UPA remained exclusive not only for the reforms initiated by the government, but also would be remembered for long for social security. The other very crucial declaration and implementation of the UPA government was 'Sixth Pay Commission' in 2006, which played a dual role. A large section of the middle-class government employed life dramatically boomed, and secondly now the market had a new consumer class, and it was large in numbers and wasn't avoidable. It attracted the MNCs to invest more in India, and further this generated jobs on a wider scale. The consumerization of the middle class increased the GDP growth, and subsequently transferred in the welfare schemes to uplift the life condition of a large section of poor people. Thus, one can say that the Congress led UPA government had felt the nerve of the Indians, and accordingly traversed by making a linkage between the new and the old ideologies of the Congress.

The 2009 general elections and the blooming Democracy – After more than two decades, finally India saw the return of the same government. Since 1989 no party has formed the government one after the other. The UPA was jubilant. Why not be? They had all the reasons to celebrate its victory, particularly when most political pundits had a very different conclusion. But the UPA didn't only win and formed the government, but in fact, the leading Congress was able to add more than sixty seats into its tally of the last Lok Sabha election. Though, still they found a few inches away from the historical majority, but that was easily manageable; and they managed it. Once again, Dr. Manmohan Singh was given responsibility of the premiership to drive the country. This election and survival of the UPA was meaningful in the sense of voting pattern also, now the new voters expected performance and work from their leaders, the funda (matter or thing) was clear, either 'work or vanish', no third choice. Definitely, the UPA government led by Dr. Manmohan was found to be satisfactory despite the very different claim and allegations against it by the oppositions; primarily by the right-wing BJP and its allies. This change in the attitude of the voters wasn't just coincidence but was the signal of a vibrant, working democracy where voters started compelling politicians to deliver the things in reality and not illusion. Therefore, by the virtue of their effective work Congress-led UPA returned to power in emphatic style. The UPA 2 started its journey for the next three years on the positive, and was rated good for its work. But somehow Congress found itself lost midway as in the last couple of years the UPA 2 government was besieged by numerous scams, high inflation and the rise in unemployment rate hit the country horizontally as well as vertically. How this happened, the UPA regime which looked to be moving, all of sudden became the titanic of its own policy? It requires introspection. Let's try and find the cause for rigorous fall and torn-out in its policies which once appreciated by one and all.

What and where do things go wrong? Certainly UPA 2 lost its way. Was it because of the social cause or economically we found ourselves on the back foot or it was security question especially after the terror attack in Mumbai or was it the corruption charges and civil disobedience movement by Anna Hazare and civil society members or was it because of the retrograde and regressive taxation policy in conjunction with general anti-avoidance rules or was it because the Rupee slipping to sixty-eight against dollar. Certainly, there isn't one cause for the Congress' ruin, but the mixture of all. If we divide the 2009-14 tenure of UPA 2, into two parts i.e., 2009-2012 and then from 2012-14, we are going to witness a very different picture.

The first three years of UPA 2 led onto the path of good economic growth, the GDP touched all time highest to 9.3%, despite that the world faced severe economic crises since 2008. The investment in infrastructure (Public and Private) was also steady through the period, only a minor slowdown was witnessed in 2011-12. Talking about the export, it had gone exceptionally well to 25% as compared to the NDA government when it remained below 15%. By now India has embraced globalization rather than shying from it. On the social issue, poverty declined miraculously from 37% in 2005-05 to 21% in 2011-12. Even the UPA 2 continues to show its performance on social issues like food security, free and compulsory education for children.

It is said that in the late summer of 2013, India witnessed a tailspin in India's economy. According to one of the official economic surveys for 2012-13, industries registered a growth rate of 3.5% and 3.1% in 2011-12 and 2012-13 respectively. When investigated, the government found that delay in implementation of the project was the cause, and this took place because of the law-and-order problems, delay in land acquisition, rehabilitation and resettlement problems, fund constraints, delay in forest and environment clearance etc. Definitely, despite speeding the pace of the liberalization policies to endorse MNCs, the UPA remained cautious toward social issues, and many times it was endured. As a result, the National GDP was reduced to around five percent. Despite the slowdown in the economic reforms including building of infrastructure, disinvestment in public sector, and privatization of public sectors, certainly, there has been remarkable growth when you compare the NDA regime of the 1999-2004 and also the post UPA 2.

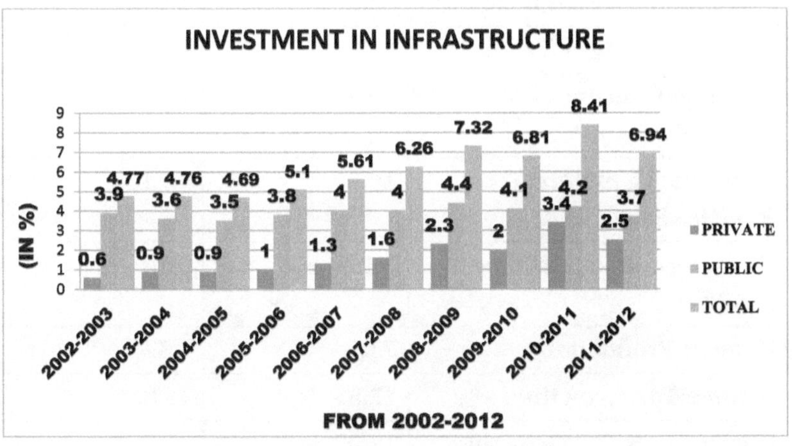

Source: Planning Commission of India.

The growth in per capita income brought in well desired consumerization in the market and also the government accumulated healthy tax in the 2009-14 tenure. Though, many economists claim that Modi's tenure had an impressive economic growth rate compared to the tenure of UPA 2. But certainly, when the things weighed and scaled on different economic indicators, it gives a very different picture of the two tenures. The figures given below reveal the other side of the picture.

THE GROWTH in UPA & Modi led NDA		
SECTOR	**Growth During 2009-2014 (in %)**	**Growth During 2014-2019 (in %)**
Domestic Scooter Sales	25.7	13.21
Domestic Tractor Sales*	15.73	4.49
Incremental Retail Loans*	22.47	19.92
Airline Passenger Traffic**	9.2	15.28
Passenger Revenues of Indian Railways#	10.81	7.32
Domestic Commercial Vehicles Sales	10.5	9.74
Consumption of Finished Steel^	7.18	5.18
Cement Production^	7.05	4.32
Income Tax Growth#	17.53	16.85
Corporation Tax Growth#	13.09	11.2
Consumption of Petroleum Products*	3.47	5.91
National Highways	5.29	8.25
*** Projection on the basis of data between Apr 2018 and Feb 2019.**		
**** Projection on the basis of data between Apr-Dec 2018**		
# Revised estimate for 2019.		
^ India Brand Equity Foundation production forecast for 2018-19		

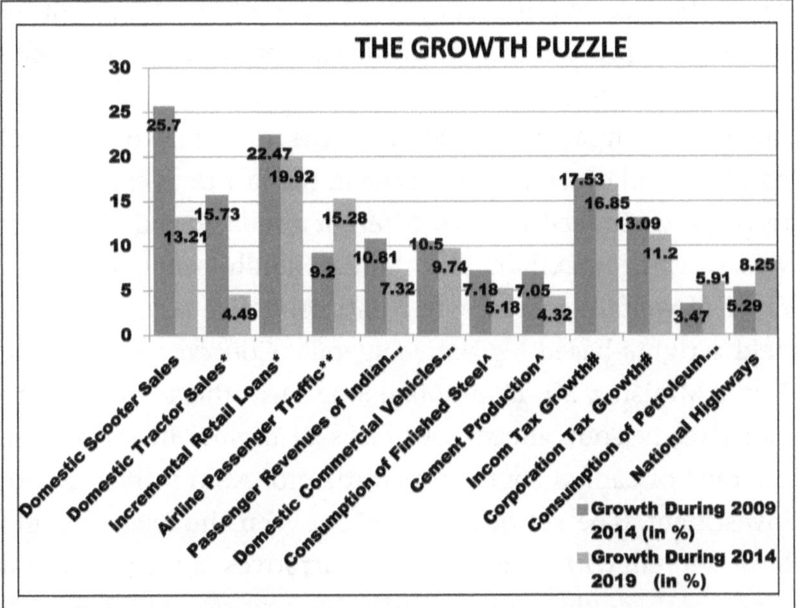

Source: *Centre for Monitoring Indian Economy; India Brand Equity Foundation, Indian Railways; Ministry of Road and Surface Transport; Budget documents; PIB' Government Data*

Though, it was true to some extent Indian economic activity slowed down in the last couple of years of UPA 2, but Congress didn't seem to be bothered much about it, instead they maintained a posture of the sphinx proud. In fact, due to the grave sink in the Indian economy, many investors surged to give up the investment in India. In the meanwhile, the Congress lagged in controlling food inflation which devoured consumer confidence. Unfortunately, the Congress had to go through social reforms too, and therefore was reluctant to take tough decisions as the poll was close by. This is what I think not exactly paralyzed the economic reform, but yes to some extent slowed for the while.

Thus, the rule of ten years of UPA, cannot be argued within the lines of pro-welfare or pro-market parties, but contained other dimensions too. Definitely, the Congress isn't a monolithic organization, at least the evidence of internal conflicts and divergent concerns in the last ten years are the testimonial. Indeed, the two different minds set and sentiment was working together. Mrs. Sonia Gandhi stood firmly in favor of welfare schemes, had anti-capitalist sentiments and held a rights-based legislative agenda. Contrary to her, The Prime Minister, Mr. Manmohan Singh was the advocator and had already gone ahead with tasks of import liberalization, removal of capital controls, privatization, and infrastructure investment. The set of divisions between the leaders could have served with two different narratives. In a jolly good time, both could produce inclusive growth, but contrary to that, in the worst of times, the same leaders would have created disarray, to lead toward unchecked corruption and absurd regulation, and undoubtedly especially the last years of the UPA 2.

The Problem in the ideological lines – Unlike the western democracy, where the parties are categorized into left and right-wing because of their economic stands. As per the theory, the right-wing party tends to believe in free markets, and minimal government, whereas the left-wing party firmly supports and stands behind to build a strong welfare state and regulated private enterprises. The two contrast ideological parties continue to contest elections largely on their contrasting economic ideologies. While in India, the narrative is very different, here more or less, the BJP is assigned the role of economic right-wing, while the secular and socially liberal, Congress is assumed to be the economic left or centrist-left, because it remained in the shell of Nehruvian socialism. That is why, Congress priority has always been related to building up an institution that nurtures the Nehruvian thoughts and mixed economy, it continued the same legacy even during the UPA rule when more or less Dr. Manmohan Singh believed to be part of the pro-capitalist camp. Whereas, BJP, right-wing continue to ride on the pro-capitalism stance, seasoned by the ingredient of pro-Hindu when and wherever it becomes the necessity to counter the opponent.

The Last but Not the Least – Did UPA turn back on globalization? A question that always puzzles, and answers cannot be toned in a black and white way. The Manmohan Government neither ended the concept of welfare state nor did he put a halt to the New Economic Policy. Perhaps, like a genius economist, he intermingled the different concepts together to fulfill the needs of the two ends. Despite the loud sounding economy, growth in employment, infrastructure etc. as compared to the previous government, the Congress saw its worst phase in the history of Indian electoral politics. it was vulnerable and had no explanation whatsoever for the debacle. It was able to grab forty-four seats, a catastrophic loss of 162 seats and dip of almost ten percent in vote sharing compared to the 2009 election. It was a blow to Congress, and rise of BJP under the leadership of former Gujarat Chief Minister and one of the responsible persons behind carnage of Muslim minority in the state, Mr. Narendra Modi.

How has the climate changed all of sudden? What factors became for the decline of Congress and for the sudden upsurge of BJP? These are some of the questions that require to be introspective for the Congress. Undoubtedly, the UPA faced the stiff challenge on two platforms – on the economic issue and another was on the political. Anyway, 2014 general election apprehended the decline of the Congress, and secondly, it was the wave in favor of the BJP's Prime Ministerial candidate Narendra Modi. The factors that devoid Congress into the strange position, despite the syncretic approach were-

1 The paucity of political leadership within Congress unfavorably influenced its electoral prospects in the 2014 general election. Indeed, Rahul Gandhi, whom the Congress reposes its faith in, has already demonstrated his lack of political acumen.

2 Whereas, Narendra Modi enjoyed a reputation as a charismatic leader, his technocratic orientation held some allure with India's business communities, while the others saw him more seasoned politician than Rahul Gandhi.

3 Much of the corporate sector, the middle class and a section of the intelligentsia had the fear with the country's political and intellectual climate, as it traditionally leaned toward the left ideology.

4 Another important factor that can be a point for the disaster of Congress was lack of leadership, that could have transported the good work of the government to the audience.

A new millennium fostered the new dynamics in tabling the eco-politics together through inclusion of capitalism and syncretism. The advent of crony capitalism representation in the form of the BJP had taken place in the Indian political arena. A new kind of political pride was shaping, Gandhian austerity was replacing in the light of meritocracy. The UPA 1 and 2, actually played a crucial role in the liberalization of the market, and unexpectedly brought the strongest economic growth since independence is traced as the enemy of free enterprise. While the opposition party was traditionally more concerned on the issue of Ram Janam Bhoomi and reconstruction of the temple. All of sudden, there was leap and bound by the same party who suddenly became the champion of "Market Reform". What an extraordinary delusion!

06

Congress: A Party of Idea and Changes

It is very well known that Indian democracy has gone through exemplary changes in thoughts and ideas in the last seventy-five years or so, and in the present scenario too, it is undergoing fundamental transformation. In fact, India has undergone and still faces a number of changes, some of which are related to systematic changes in the nature of electoral competition, a significant increase in the number of middle-class people, and the development and penetration of mass media and social media. These phenomena acted as a teaser and influencer for Indian society. The last two decades remained miraculous for the right-wing BJP, who overwhelmingly were able to establish massive support of all sections of Hindu society; perhaps it laid down the significant gain by polarizing the people on religious lines by solidly cashing in on the breach between the Hindus and minorities; Muslims. Under the leadership of present prime minister Narendra Modi, the BJP was able to garnish its ideology by mixing up the slogan of "development." Thus, altering the political landscape further marginalized the Congress; in fact, the left front or the left parties also are decimated, and the state-level parties, who saw the positive growth since 1989, have seen a decline in their strength in most of the states; in fact, many of them have not only shrunk their popular support but are almost on the verge of decay. These changes in Indian politics are taking us away from the "multi-party system," and it is alarming for Indian democracy.

In this year when India is celebrating its seventy-five years of independence, it is an important time to assess the role of political parties in shaping the country's democracy in the rapidly changing political landscape. Of course, modern democracies are beyond imagination without the political parties, as they are the epicenter that serves as the nerve between citizens and the state, and in a democratic country, the parties act as the backbone of democracy. India isn't barren of that, as its policies, programs, and ideologies are the reflection of the society, and the society also adheres to the values of democracy in the atmosphere established by the political parties.

In Part 1, we tried to cover the different phases of Congress from 1885 to 2014. A long and vital period of pre-independent India was covered, where Congress at one stage seemed to act as a safety valve for the British government. The early stages of the Indian National Congress had been a period of preaching and pleading for reforms and getting some kind of compensation for the elite Indians. But consequently, more or less, they emphasized the issues of the farmers, students, and other sections of the Indian society of the time. it was also the time when Congress was amalgamated with leaders of diverse political orientations, from Western-educated and egalitarian-minded social elites to conservative and orthodox Hindus and nationalist Muslims. The scores of years of the early twentieth century would be remembered for the acute ideological conflict among the forces of moderate and radical within the Congress. More or less, this ideological conflict remained throughout the independent struggle; sometimes it took the form of an inner-party struggle that became sharp, while there were times when it seemed poised to be steady.

Undoubtedly, in the first half of the twentieth century, Congress was covered in a garland of vivid colours. In other words, Congress was an umbrella party for various ideas. But there was a time when the umbrella structure acted as a curse or a moribund force for the Congress, while on other occasions it became the sublime force explicating the Indian national movement's struggle on the higher stage.

The sudden assassination of Mahatma Gandhi by a treacherous right-wing conspirator, Nathuram Godse, was a shock not only for the Congress but for the entire nation. For a moment, it looked like there would be an end to the Hindutva thought in the Congress, but the secular leaders like Jawaharlal Nehru and others weren't at all biased against any ideology, till it benefitted and united the country, but now the country was vigilant. Nevertheless, the Congress remained the omnibus for various ideologies. In fact, leaders like Sardar Vallabhbhai Patil, who was a staunch Hindu nationalist, played a crucial role in the Congress and condemned Mahatma Gandhi's assassination as cowardly. Perhaps he remained Deputy Prime Minister and Home Minister in the first Congress cabinet after the independence of India. Was it the modesty or duty of Congress? Or, was it the compulsion that bound a diverse country like India, where no electoral majority is cast in stone and no ideological hegemony would have enjoyed the permanence? Whatever the reason, Congress is certainly ahead of the curve with its coalition of ideologies. It wasn't the first time that Congress embraced the versatile shades of ideologies together, but we have seen that all through India's national movement struggle against colonial rule. Perhaps the implications of such a method of consolidating the broader ideologies enabled the Congress to share a platform of vivid ideas and thoughts with a changing world and also be able to furnish significant growth in the organizational structure and further enhance the deeper root in philosophy.

Today, when Congress, the old monk, is celebrating its 137 years of foundation and India has already completed the journey of seventy-five years of independence, it becomes quite important to assess the role of political parties, including the Congress, in shaping the country's democracy. Certainly, one must remember that modern democracies cannot be imagined without the political parties, as the parties are the tool that serve the nerve that links citizens and the state in three critical domains-

1   It serves as channels of voicing individual grievances.
2   Act as vehicles of political ambitions and
3   It is a platform for interest groups to forge political settlements.

When we are set to understand the thoughts and the transformations that have taken place in Congress over the years, we must analyze and investigate in light of the political evolution of the country and how the political parties emerge in India. It also becomes crucial, without being adamant, to understand how Indian parties harvest democracy compared to other countries, particularly western democracies.

Certainly, the political parties around the world have their own organizational lives, but at the same time, they are also nested in a party system. In fact, the building of a political party largely depends on the historical, social, and cultural aspects of a particular country. Indeed, no two countries with social, historical, and cultural differences would have the same kind of political party system and parties. For instance, the parties of the United States of America cannot be similar to Indian parties either in ideology or in practice. Both nations consist of different notions and are dictated by very different terms. In the USA, the nation-building process wasn't similar to that in India. In fact, the structure of politics is dissimilar, though both countries believe in democracy and appreciate the federal structure. But when it comes to the question of practice, the USA practices "coming together," while India upholds "holding together." In the same way, we pursue the multi-party system, while many countries in the European block and even the USA have a two-party system instead of a multi-party system. To understand further, we need to analyze the party system in India.

The evolution of the Party System in India – Predominantly, India is a bouquet of diversity in all its forms. We have diversity in beliefs and practices, culturally we stand very differently, we have more than hundreds of languages and dialects, even the food habits, dresses and rituals and customs also change while crossing from one region to another. Such factors are very complex in the formation of political parties. This complexity arises from the complex nature of the society. But at the same time this phenomenon drives the party with aspiration too. The different ideas that emerge from the diverse society helps the Indian political parties to nurture the new idea, and that makes the parties of two different ethnicities differ from each in ideology and practice, but at the same time binds the nation together, while working in the same structure.

In India, the party's formation takes place to a large extent on ethnic grounds. Currently, we have as many as six national parties, but out of those, at least four are limited to only the areas among their own language and culture background, while the two parties, the Congress and the BJP, have national-based structures, i.e., from Jammu-Kashmir to Kanyakumari in the north-south direction, and from east-west, these two parties have substantial presence all the way from Arunachal Pradesh to the Rann of Kuchh (Gujarat). Why is it so? The answer lies in the population composition of India's diverse society.

It's not that the other parties don't have an all-India vision; in fact, the narrative of the past and present clearly demonstrates that there were and are a number of parties who have the vision to build the nation. but couldn't extend their mass base support beyond their own regional pockets. The Communist parties were the other group that expanded its territories, but that too in a limited way, and that too is the story of the last century. Unfortunately, the new millennium was a blow for them, as their mass base and pockets seemed to be shrinking drastically, but that doesn't mean they are totally wiped out. Their existence is still visible, but it is slowly and gradually losing its shine. The other major national party, the Congress, holds around twenty percent of its votes, though compared to the old Congress, yes, their position has gone to dearth from the skyscraper. To search for nuances, let's go back to the nascence to understand the formation of political parties and how they are able to endure themselves in different circumstances.

It would be wise to understand and start with a basic question, that is, the ideological framework on which electoral contests in India are mounted. And secondly, how have the very "ideas of India" shaped the country's political parties, including the grand old party, Congress? While going into the research work, there has been various trends that we come across and observes which needed to be shared-

1   The foremost and significant aspect that strikes about the Indian party politics, since independence is, they seem to be rooted deeply with ideological bounds and that is why any divisions on the role of the state influences the changes. In fact, the different ideas of state intervention in social norms, or whether to provide special treatment to the disadvantaged groups have long historic lineages; it takes us back into India's national movement i.e.., in the first half of the twentieth century.

2   In the ideological space, the Indian political parties can be marked into three different folds – an era of Congress domination, this goes back to the national movement to almost the second last decades of the twentieth century, then a transition period of multi-party competition by the last decade of the previous millennium, and the new millennium gave knock on right-wing dominance in the form of the BJP, shrinking space for all kinds of ideologies and parties, including the Congress. If one goes into the nuances of the transition, it is understandable that it isn't just limited to representation in the political composition of the legislature but has expanded toward rural and backward caste dominance. In other words, Indian politics has become more representative of its social structures than ever before.

3   India has witnessed, there are many ways in which the party forms, one was before the independence and the next four in post-independence respective phases in the

period of last seventy-five years. Nevertheless, in the Indian scenario, the party formation is interesting, as it takes place quite often. But very few parties survive beyond the two or three electoral political cycles. It is very interesting to see that more and more parties rise due to opportunistic tendency and egoistic approach of the leaders in parties, and not due to the ideological differences. And consequences are in the form of splits within the party occasionally. In fact, a large number of parties do resemble each other in their organizational structure, functioning as well as in ideology, this also makes them easier to merge into their liking party without much fuss. The centralization of political parties also hampers the unity within the party and the circumstances unable them to respond toward societal grievances.

In a nutshell, India's political parties act as vanguards for various societal forces, and in some regard, they achieve success in some arenas while falling short in others. Indeed, the diversity of India's political system means that no electoral majority is cast in stone, and no ideological hegemony is permanence.

The glimpses of the traversal stage – In the early stage after India's independence, Congress dominated the political arena from 1952 to 1964, it more looked like a 'one-party system', than a multi-party system. It evolved like a big umbrella under which all communities and ideologies got a place. Though, there were many other parties that contested against Congress, but probably acted just as a pressure group.

The other phase began in Indian politics after the demise of Jawaharlal Nehru. This period continued from 1964 to

1977. The 1967 election was a threat to the dominance of the Congress party. It was the phase where Congress failed to secure majorities in eight states, further reducing its seats to an all-time low. This phase can be called the "transition phase" of Indian politics, as regional parties started emerging in the country. Ironically, despite the challenges from everywhere, Indira Gandhi was able to establish her supremacy both within the party and in the government. But very soon, things went out of the hands of the Congress when a successful movement led by the opposition brought an end to Indira's regime and thoughts, though it was only for a short span of time.

Nevertheless, the new coalition brought a wave of ideology and hope for the Indians. This was the first time in Indian electoral history when people were looking for change. This was against the rising tyranny, corruption, and bureaucratic rule of the Congress. Though many of the parties that joined hands had no ideological consensus except for the same foe, the honeymoon among them couldn't last for long, and a debacle came by the end of 1979. Congress's ideology once again gained power. Anyhow, the period between 1977 and 1980 was the time for the new ideology to emerge and the sharpening of inner-party conflict.

1980–1989 witnessed a tussle between the Congress at the center and the newly emerging regional parties at the state level. It was the time when Congress brought a change in working methods and frivolously used the president's rule in many states under Article 356 to curtail the voices of the opposition parties, who were emerging and strengthening in various states of the country.

The murmuring of the multi-party system was already on the table since the beginning of the 1980s; the Congress was getting weaker in many states as new regional parties were emerging, but only the right opportunity was required, so it was waiting for the right time. No later than 1989, the various opposition parties grasped the opportunity, including the BJP and the left front, to make sure to establish a non-congress government, though this couldn't continue for a long time. but thereafter, a new trend emerged in the Indian political scenario: the formation of the coalition government. This new phenomenon was the beginning of the multi-party system and coalition politics. This trend merely came into existence because of the growth of regional parties. This also led to the emergence of caste – and community-based parties. It was the time when the regional parties filled the vacuum of protecting the minorities, which earlier was done by the Congress; as a result, the minorities, Dalits, and OBCs scattered from the Congress and showed loyalty to their caste-based parties. But the coalition politics empowered the regional parties, and was able to strengthen federalism. Since 1996, several regional parties have been sharing power at the national level, either with the UPA or as constituents of the NDA.

Swinging of thoughts and programs – How do we see Congress? Do we figure any major difference between the Congress of pre-independence and post-independence? Or whether it would be right to analyze Congress in pre and post. Or would there be another way to understand the changes within Congress? Definitely, some basic, but relevant questions take us to consider about the reshuffling of ideas and thought in the Congress, and at the same time we accumulate the picture of the changes taking place in the Congress and overall, its policies. Undoubtedly, policy and thought are the integral part of each other, when one is changed, the other also takes a new form. And this has happened many times in the Congress too.

Since its formation, Congress has more or less remained an umbrella party, accommodating various different ideologies together. This method of mobilizing the Indian people was unique, and many times it bore fruit for the Congress as well as for the Indian national movement. The nascence of the second decade of the twentieth century saw the arrival of Mahatma Gandhi, and Congress was credited with his thoughts in the next few decades. Interestingly, the arrival of Gandhi on the political horizon of the national movement of India urged Congress to make several changes in its thinking and implementation. The party that only acted as the bargainer till the end of the first decade of the twentieth century suddenly geared itself for the movement against British hegemony. One can say that it was a transformational stage for the Congress as well as Indian politics. The magic wand of "non-violence" appealed to a larger section of the Indian masses, though it is also equally true that non-violence works differently for different people and communities. But for sure, Mahatma Gandhi was able to awaken the hibernating Indian masses. The Civil Disobedience to Quit India Movement that covered the vast pan India was significant in mobilizing the people as well as in tarnishing the roots of the British, who claimed that their sun never sets. This was the period when Congress, under the indirect leadership of Mahatma Gandhi, heightened the intensity of the broader Indian population.

Certainly, it was the time when Congress showed flexibility and rigidity both in its political stances and in its leadership. The challenge for the Congress was to jointly work with the moderates and radicals who were fragmented from each other on the issues practice and the thoughts, and secondly, advent of Jawaharlal Nehru brought the principles of 'Nehruvian Socialism and "Secularism," which was unacceptable for the right-wing leaders within the Congress. Indeed, these differences unfortunately took the Congress toward repercussions, but sometimes tussling in thought even leads the thing toward a glossy future. In a real sense, the set of conflicts hampered little but nourished the party significantly and in the healthiest form to fight against British rule in the pre-independence era. This was the time when Congress had an opportunity to transit itself from narrow sectarian views and shape itself to be the party of diverse Indian society. The broadness of thought compelled a stalwart Hindu leader like Shyama Prasad Mukherjee to join the cabinet of Jawaharlal Nehru as the Minister for Industry and Supply. Even at several occasions, the Congress and Mahatma Gandhi tried to negotiate with the Muslim League, and he successfully ended up making an alliance in favour of the Khilaft Movement so that the Muslim-Hindu unity together would help strengthen the national movement.

Thus, it had been recognized that the Congress, under the leadership of Mahatma Gandhi and Jawaharlal Nehru, and even, to some extent, Sardar Vallabh Bhai Patel, a staunch Hindu nationalist who was part of the Congress, never feared to float new ideas and dared to go with changes. Despite the majority of the Congress in the constituent assembly, Congress made sure that dissenting voices must be heard and be part of the constituent assembly so that the constitution of India must have all the colors of diversity that are found on Indian soil, and that is the reason we were able to frame one of the most unique constitutions in the world. Whatever the case, in the pre-independence and early stages of free India, the Congress always remained a party of the right-centre-left.

Later in the years after the independence of India and the framing of the Indian Constitution, the parties had to go ahead with building a modern India. The Congress formed the first elected government of independent India, with Jawaharlal Nehru as the first Prime Minister. It was a difficult time for India; still haunted by the partition tragedy, the economy was hovering while the society was fragmented into pieces; altogether, we were in a dismal state. To advance the country and its people was a daunting task for any government, especially when many political analysts and leaders of other countries believed that India would be divided into bits and pieces. In a nutshell, India had fallen into the grip of darkness without any kind of support, but Nehru, with his broad vision, not only drew India out of its pathetic stage but also took it to the heights of making it a self-reliant India. Here, it becomes important to assimilate the stated statement of Mahatma Gandhi. It was stated a day before his assassination where he said, "The "Congress has won political freedom, but it has yet to win economic freedom." He further added, "Social and moral freedoms are harder to achieve than political freedom." Definitely, he was right, and early Congress would have felt the heat of that. But despite the odd circumstances, the Congress made all efforts to build a self-reliant nation. Though it wasn't easy, it was Nehru's socialism in collaboration with Gandhian principles and Sardar Vallabh Bhai Patel's nationalistic approach that made the daunting task possible. It was only under the notion of "leaders and thinkers" that India was able to march ahead and bring astonishing changes in a short period of time. India's progress was against all predictions and forecasts. Despite such proclamations, there is yet another argument that goes up in the air against the ideological collaboration theory. There is a view that the Congress' predicament basically lies in its formation. Such thinkers express their disapproval about such an impiety alliance of thoughts. According to them, the Congress arose from the womb of an enlightened jamboree, and therefore, instead of having one ideology, the Congress had several ideologies that worked together at a time. The borrowed legacy of multi-dimensional ideology also had its reflection in Nehru's government, which had diverse political orientations that included western-educated and egalitarian-minded social elites as well as conservative Hindus, nationalist Muslims, etc. Whatever may be right, we cannot express it with full authority, but certainly Congress and its leadership were able to tackle the challenges that India was confronting after independence with courage and wisdom. Without a doubt, it can be said that it was the Congress and its leaders' efforts that enabled the country to assimilate every bit of dust and move toward building an economically, socially, culturally, and politically strong nation. In fact, things didn't die only at that juncture, but rather rose to change the momentum of the country, and still the legacy of the past is held by all the major parties, despite the fact that they are right-center-left, but more often than not, in the formation of the government, the real roots of society are exhibited. A glimpse of the same was also observed in the era of Mrs. Indira Gandhi, who was considered to be centrist-left, whereas the Janata Party and Janata Dal governments also remained exemplary examples of the accumulation of ideologies and political culture.

India has crossed seventy-odd years of electoral politics and seventy-five years of independence, and in these long years, it has fluttered all shades of ideologies. The political parties' journey started from the Congress (centrist party) to the BJP (right-wing party), and in between for a short span, we saw the ingredients of various ideologies into a party like the Janata Party (1977–1979) and Janata Dal (1989–1991). Besides the major parties that ruled over the years in the center, there has been a cluster of regional parties that resemble themselves with their own regional and linguistic identity. These are the groups of various flavors that occasionally come together and then depart, making disarray at occasions, but in the last three decades, the regional and smaller parties have played a sublime role in the Indian political arena in their respective states or regions, and even at several occasions they came up strongly in the center and made their importance recognized in the power game of numbers.

For years, however, the Congress was synonymous with the idea of India, but in the present scenario, the idea of India has undergone a drastic change. Now, Nehruvian socialism has given way to Hinduism, or Hindu nationalism. Despite the massive setback in the last few years, Congress has always been more of a broad national movement than just a political party or a party of a religious majority. Perhaps it has provided a broader platform for people from different social backgrounds. It believes in change but with continuity and a human face, and therefore always stresses an economically prosperous, socially just, politically united, and harmonious India. The last seventy years of Congress are known for their comprehensive and continuous change, and these changes came according to the needs of the people. Here, the glimpses of the changes that has been brought in different phases by the Congress is narrated-

- In the decade of 1950s, Congress was working for land reforms, community development, the public sector and working toward the growth of education, agriculture, industries and other infrastructure.
- While in the 1960s and 70s, it attacked directly and mercilessly on poverty, and urged for nationalization of banks to fulfill the demands of the small and cottage industries.
- In the 80s, the Congress emphasized on science and technology to meet the challenges of the 21st century.
- The year of the 1990s is marked for the need of economic reforms and liberalization, that included privatization, it was done to accelerate the economic growth, so that India could compete and cope with the changing world.

Over the years, the Congress has gone through various stages and brought significant changes to its thinking. Such changes were foreseen in the impact of the social transformation that occurred in different phases during post-independence India. In fact, the changes in thoughts and practice weren't only in Congress; they were in the entire machinery of the political party system. And therefore, we can recognize Indian democracy as sui generis, as it is just a by-product of institutional design that accidentally emerged from the contradictory forces rooted in Indian society. Indian political parties play an important and crucial role by acting as a platform for these societal forces without being biased or adamant, no matter what the outcome may be, but certainly their agility and adaptability have kept everyday politics energized and on its toes for everyone.

07

Crisis of Leadership in Congress

Is the dynasty a hurdle in the development of leadership or is there some other reason that stops the blooming of a new leadership or such issues have emerged as a hype? Whatever may be, certainly Congress is going through a leadership crisis. The crisis of leadership within Congress isn't a problem of the last few years, but it takes us back to the assassination of Mrs. Indira Gandhi; a stalwart leader of seventies. In fact, Mrs. Gandhi seized the leadership in the Congress from the throats of other established leaders either by expelling them from the party or creating a split in the party. This has been a regular phenomenon during sixties and seventies when many senior leaders and staunch Congressmen were expelled from the party because they raised their voice against Mrs. Gandhi. Earlier, in the book it has been brought among the readers how Gandhi split the party to appease herself. It was the time when Congress meant Indira, and Indira was Congress. will it be appropriate to say that Indira's approach was the key factor in the decline of the Congress? or there had been other factors that played pivotal roles in the development of the leadership crisis. Whatever may be the reason, but for sure at present Congress is triggered with a series of problems, and one of the majors is the leadership. Where does the problem lie? Is it in the burrow of dynasty or the problem of ideology that curtails the possibility of leadership beyond the Nehru-Gandhi family. Or, are there any other sources? We shall try to reach closer to the problem.

The recent years of Congress have been the story of sorrow and disappointment in terms of its organizational structure as well as Congress immensely facing the leadership crisis from top to bottom. In fact, such a problem didn't reflect for the first time in Congress. As earlier already stated, it found itself in sought of disorder, but it was able to come out and strengthened itself either by the charismatic leadership or at occasions because devoted cadres supplied oxygen to Congress to fight against unprecedented circumstances to avoid further damage to the party. But today within the Congress has changed abundantly, the problem of leadership isn't just limited at the center level or the state level, in fact, the cancer has gone deep to the local level. The party is facing upheavals in almost all the states units, even rumbling is there within the local units of the party in the states like Chhattisgarh, Rajasthan and Kerala. While at the national level, the group of twenty-three senior Congress leaders (G-23) has been vocal with demands of structural reform in the party. Now, Azad and Sibal have become raincoats, and finally the election for the highest post has made the voices down. Now, which way things will move in future, it won't be wise to discuss that right now. definitely after the election of president, the situation which continued to linger for some time because of Rahul Gandhi uninterested in the post and Sonia Gandhi herself was only interim president, this led the things in the party for the worst. This vacuum created anguish within the rank and file of the Congress.

Internal Strife in the Party – For now, the Indian National Congress looks to be a "sinking ship"; by now for many of us it is an open and end case. Yet it is a bit astonishing to think when it comes to how far the political party has come down. After all, the Congress party had a long legacy, not very far when the history of Congress ran almost parallel with the history of India. Indeed, the leaders of Congress were naturally the leaders of India, and when go back into colonial India and building of national movement, we come across that a larger part of the movement was owed the existence to congress, of course, Congress wasn't just a political party than, but an umbrella organization where different schools of thought co-existed together. Despite the bi-polar ideologies and practice, not much crisis was experienced in the leadership. Indeed, the Congress of national movement was very different from the Congress after the 80s. The organizational structure of Congress was deep-rooted and entrenched.

But unfortunate for the Congress that it couldn't uphold the ideals of then, perhaps found itself at a murky stage in the later years of the last century. The Congress which dominated the Central as well as the states, it was mainly due to the fact that people voted in the name of the Congress; a Congress that brought freedom for the country. But unfortunately, the hope of the people tarnished with the decaying of the decades, and passing of the years. Gradually, the people realized that the Congress is sick of nepotism, and corruption.

The first jolt came to Congress when Jawaharlal Nehru died in 1964. For the first time within the Congress raised the question: Who after Nehru? His death created a vacuum in the political space, though Congress positioned Lal Bahadur Shastri, but not for long, as he died in 1966. His death brought the Congress on its knees, as the inner party struggle arose and increased further when Congress lost as many as eight states in 1967 elections. The things didn't stop there, in fact, seven members of Indira Gandhi's cabinet were also defeated, in six states the party's president also lost, while in four states the sitting Chief Minister lost their seats. It was for the first time Congress seemed to be losing its touch; a sign of first ever break. Eventually, an inner leadership fight led the party to split into many factions, of which some merged with the Janata Party during the emergency to challenge Indira's regime.

Despite the challenges, Mrs. Indira Gandhi emerged as a strong and decisive leader within Congress. In fact, her leadership brought a decisive victory against Pakistan in 1971. This victory provided space for Indira as well as Congress to make a comeback, despite the division in the party. Nevertheless, Indira Gandhi was a Charismatic leader, and had potential to change the tide in her favor; and she was able to show her superiority on other leaders as well as opposition parties at several occasions.

But sometimes, the unchecked power becomes problematic, and it happened to congress and to its supreme leader Mrs. Indira, when she suspended all democratic rights of the people and concentrated all the powers in her own hand; it was said "Indira is India, and India is Indira". But it is also true that many Congress senior leaders like Kamraj, Morarji Desai etc. became raincoats, and later they combined together to form the government at the Centre. It was for the first time that both people and political parties believed that there could be an alternative to the Congress. Despite the early blow in the Congress in the late and early seventies, Mrs. Indira Gandhi established her leadership in two ways; either by siding dissent leaders or dividing the party to have the leadership. In these ways, she was able to strengthen herself as a legitimate leader of the Congress, but contrary to that her action caused the split and weakened the party structure. the two of the things went parallel to each other.

Leadership Crisis of the Recent Phase – In the latest inner conflicts that emerged within the Congress party, it left the Congress in an unpleasant defeat in Punjab. The inner conflict between the former chief minister Amarinder Singh and Navjot Singh Sidhu, finally brought a raged defeat for the Congress in Punjab, and paved the path for Aam Aadmi Party (AAP) to grab the power in Punjab. This defeat was humiliating for the Congress. Besides the defeat, the Congress also lost one of its stalwart leaders in Punjab. But Punjab isn't the first and last state that is facing such turmoil within the party. Chhattisgarh is another state that Congress rules, here too there has been turmoil within the party. There is a tussle between the Chief Minister Bhupesh Baghel and T. S. Singh Deo, though the central leadership brought temporary relief for the Chief Minister, but the problems have not been abated nor been settled. Another significant state from the point of perspective for the Congress is Rajasthan which is a bed of thorns for the party leadership. The state continues to witness tussle between the two giant figures of Rajasthan politics; Ashoka Gehlot, the chief minister of the state at present and Deputy Chief Minister Sachin Pilot. Several times both the leaders of the Congress were called to Delhi for negotiation, but all hard work of the central authority seems to go in vain as both the camps look to be hostile against one another. the other state that is facing the leadership problem is Uttarakhand where Congress came up with peculiar method to resolve the problem of inner conflict within the party, appointment of three state president, but implication of this method brought state congress into deeper crisis, and for now the Congress no better than a fragmented party; without any leader to control and regulate the party.

In other states where the Congress party has been out of power for several years, in those states also Congress doesn't seem to build up, rather Congress looks to be in a dismal situation. The Goa unit of the Congress also sticks to the same narrative, where Luizinho Faleiro, an ex-Chief Minister and a seven-time MLA, left the party and joined Trinamool Congress. It was an unbelievable dent on the Congress. The story doesn't end here for the Congress. Such dissident voices in the Congress reveal the dissatisfaction within the party, perhaps there are various issues for such a decisive decision, but one of the majors is the appointment of leaders. This issue again and again has been brought under the consideration of the Congress Working Committee (CWC) by G-23.

Another state that requires it to be addressed is Karnataka, where the PCC president of Karnataka, D. K. Shivakumar as well as Siddaramaiah who installed themselves in the position as fighters and have taken on the ruling BJP on every issue by mobilizing party members on the streets, but then both leaders are engaged in ugly power tussles, and unfortunately the central leadership has turned itself to deaf ear. The other states' stories are very much similar, and at any hour the resentment can turn into rebellion against the party.

It is true that in recent years the Congress current leadership in states failed to contain multi-layers of dissatisfaction and resentment. In fact, its own organizational design has been ineffective in building the party at the grassroots. Perhaps, now the party is heavily dependent upon only a few handful leaders to bring out the party from its disarray situation. But the question that worries, isn't one, but many and those are also in layers. The Central leadership also needs to be scanned for the failure of Congress in recent years. Gradual decline of Congress strength began in the late 90s, when it lost the power at Centre as well as disappointment in the heartland of India. Though it was able to grasp the power in 1991, Narasimha Rao became the Non-Gandhi Prime Minister after Lal Bahadur Shastri, but Congress continued to lose the ground and as a result from 1996 to 2004, it remained out of power.

Mrs. Sonia Gandhi's arrival to Congress was a legitimate test for her efficiency, and this proved promising for the Congress, as her leadership brought back the life within Congress, and as a result Congress succeeded in forming government in many states, and later in 2004 against vilify remarks of political analysts, Congress in the leadership of Mrs. Sonia Gandhi turned the table with an amazing victory and formed the government in the Centre, and thereafter continued to be in power for consecutive two tenures, from 2004 to 2014. A series of victories for the Congress in states and two consecutive victories in the Centre brought confidence in the Congressmen for Mrs. Sonia Gandhi as a leader of the party. And why not so? The Congress in her leadership was able to stand as a united party for as much as sixteen years, leaving tidbits like Sharad Panwar, Sangama, Mamata Banerjee and few others who left the party on different issues. However, Congress advanced despite the challenges emerging against the party from its own men who later found their own respective parties; but remained the alliance partner of Congress in United Progressive Alliance (UPA).

The failure of Congress in the past two general elections i.e., 2014 and 2019, had been a massive blow in terms of ideology as well as organizationally to Congress. BJPs massive and ruthless campaign against the congress, shattered the entire system of Congress as a party. In fact, in some of the states like Uttar Pradesh, Bihar, West Bengal etc. the party was on the brink for, say, three decades, and the last two elections only made its condition worse than the earlier. The defeats of the Congress in most of the state assembly elections added to its worry, and wherever the party able to get majority to form the government, it was the BJP hunted the Congress's men, and as a result of that the Congress was shrewdly toppled by the BJP; Madhya Pradesh, Karnataka and Goa are the living example where the Congress MLAs betrayed their own party and shifted their loyalty toward BJP. Moreover, it is also felt that most of the Congress leaders failed to understand the system of BJP's political dominance; ideologically as well as organizationally. Nor the leaders showed any interest to lead the party from the front.

A Juggernaut Central Leadership of the Congress – Who is responsible for the rampage in the Congress? A very simple question, but a complex one when it comes to the question of resolving. It isn't the Congress where dissent doesn't raise the flag of rebellion, nor it is for the first time in the history of Congress. Then where does the problem lie? Would it be right to blame the second leadership or only those Congressmen who raised dissent voices are to be pinned? Yes, it has been as transparent as glass that Congress faced a crisis of leadership and conflict among the leaders more at the state units than at the top. The reason lies in the ways that Central leadership tried to resolve the conflict.

It is also true that despite continuous defeat for the Congress in the Lok Sabha elections and State legislative elections, it still holds around 20% of vote share at the national level. Despite years of continuous defeat, the Congress is still around which in itself is a testament of its strength. But one cannot deny or reject the crisis that is faced by the Congress; especially in terms of repeated election defeats one after another at both the levels. Where does the problem lie? Definitely, it is the crisis of the current leadership that is required to be corrected with urgent effect. It looks like congress is caught in a traffic jam behind a sleeping driver. It is not the question of election defeat or success, but something more important and significant thing is missing, and that is the clarity to move forward.

Further, the Congress leadership doesn't know how to utilize the resources, manpower and votes base that the party still dominates. Leadership doesn't mean only a bunch of Gandhi's family members, but leadership contains the broader circle of people that hold responsible positions within the party from top to bottom of the party structure. In fact, there isn't a doubt that Gandhi family members are the most populous figures among the Congress leaders, and whenever the Congress stuck, it has been the Gandhi family leadership that brought the Congress out of the difficult times.

As earlier it has been pointed out that the Congress problem isn't Gandhi's family, contrary to that most of the political analysts still believe that they act as an oxygen for the Congress. Then where did the Congress fail?

The most important problem is that the Congress leadership has forgotten that it is a political party which has to motivate its ranks and files to secure power to implement its program. definitely, a political party cannot be a mere club of people. In no way, one can be accepted as a leader who doesn't wish to be leader. Mahatma Gandhi can be an exemplary example who had no desire for power, but was a consummate leader who devoted his life for his ideals and political goals.

Today, when Congress is in an isolating position or by far shrinking its base, it becomes quite necessary as well as essential for the Congress leadership to make themselves free from the haunches. It is the time when the leadership needs to break the shackle that they have positioned themselves over the years in a certain homogeneity in terms of their social positioning. Here, I don't mean to sing dirge for the Congress, obviously, a big no. But for sure, the Congress needs an immediate overhaul. Sooner or later, the leadership of Congress has to initiate the overhaul of the party, and if not done immediately then the Congress has to pay the price for it. Thou, ideology and outlook remain alive by entering into the soul of other parties, but Congress as an organization and as a political party meet its end. However, the historical legacy of the party is secure as long as the Republic of India thrives.

Nehru-Gandhi Family: Compulsion or Need for the Congress – Many senior Congress leaders are abandoning the party, some who are left are scattered by the party performance in the recent elections as well as organizational taboos and the leadership's dismal approach. Ghulam Nabi Azad, a staunch Congressman from Jammu & Kashmir in his resignation letter alleged the party organization is in a shamble, and chiefly because of "new coterie of inexperienced sycophants", obviously he targeted Mr. Rahul Gandhi for his reluctant efforts. In fact, this allegation wasn't for the first time, over the years after the collateral defeat in 2014 Lok Sabha election, both in terms of electoral as well as organizational decline, Congress leadership, particularly Rahul Gandhi's ability was scanned and put to question by some top leaders of the Congress. Although the spate of resignations is a recent phenomenon, as a result of leading governments in nine states, the Congress fortunes have plummeted to just in the present scenario – Chhattisgarh and Rajasthan. This created panic even for some Congressmen. However, the staunch consensus within the party, especially among young cadres is to go with the Gandhi family still dominates. But there is a problem, as Mrs. Sonia Gandhi who had remained an undisputed top leader and the president of the Congress, though her political beginning had been reluctant, but once she took the charge after that never looked back. Her deteriorating health issue in the recent phase remained an obstacle for her as well as for the Congress. But still she is the most popular leader among the Congress.

But where do the problems really lie? Why is the Congress on the verge of decline both organizationally and ideologically? There can be various arguments, but most significant that I guess is the presence of inefficient leaders at key positions. Many young Congressmen are of the view that several politicians in the party were chosen and groomed during Mrs. Indira Gandhi's time, and they were trained as efficient ministers, who had exposure to the minister's office, but weren't good in field work. The young blood feel that the old brigades aren't efficient enough to challenge Modi wave, as the old leaders are trapped in a quagmire that demands a different skill altogether. The cozy cabins aren't going to work for

Congress to establish itself. In fact, they are also aware about it, and therefore they are looking to make an escape from the party, but before that they sling mud on individuals, and perhaps, Rahul Gandhi is suit enough for such humiliation, as he isn't able to prove himself like other Nehru-Gandhi family members.

"Perhaps, Rahul Gandhi's reluctant approach to take the leadership has replicated the model of his mother and grandmother to lead the party," wrote Heidelberg University professor Rahul Mukherji. In fact, his quitting from the presidential post of the Congress gave the opportunity to other political parties and leaders to defame him as politically inept and rudderless. Right now, Congress party is in the revamping stage, and most of the leaders who are in 60s and 70s are disgruntled because they find themselves mismatch in the new setup; it is flashback of 60s when Indira Gandhi took the charge of the party and governance, and several Congress leaders who were senior couldn't digest Indira's seizing the post. Today also, such leaders are there who are exhibiting their dissatisfaction with Rahul Gandhi.

Finally after twenty-four years Mrs. Sonia Gandhi has stepped down from the president of Congress, and through election Mr. Mallikarjun Kharge has been elected a new president of the Congress. Though, Gandhi family remained away from giving their support any of the two candidates; but as some people believe that their secret blessing was with Mr. Mallikarjun Kharge. Now, one has to wait and watch whether the new president has enough guts to work freely or require the blessing of 10 Janpath. Time will tell the fortune of him. Meanwhile, Mr. Rahul Gandhi finally showed courage to take some initiative by organizing "Bharat Jodo Campaign", but how far will it work and what political and organization benefit Congress will reap; that is in the womb of future. definitely we shall discuss the campaign led by Rahul Gandhi in a separate chapter.

137 years old Grand Congress party is going through the worst phase in the present scenario, several staunch Congress leaders have turned raincoats, whereas some are waiting for an appropriate opportunity to cross the party. In the span of eight years, it dramatically lost two consecutive Lok Sabha elections, and in fact found itself to be one of the worst places in the number of Lok Sabha seats, while it has been confined only to two states – Rajasthan and Chhattisgarh. The Hindi heartland which contributes the majority of Lok Sabha seats, Congress has lost its ground, and near future is blink because Congress organization is very weak and scattered. In states, the Congress leadership continues to make the situation more embarrassed for the party because of inner fight among the leaders, instead of fighting unitedly against the reactionary ideology of BJP. Certainly, the senior leaders aren't ready to give the passage to the younger generation, and this often leads to a leadership crisis. The problem lies in the Congress leadership, especially in the case of Rahul Gandhi, who oftenly encircled by the leaders who do not possess the political acumen. This often ditches the leadership quality of the Congress. But contrary to all these factors, still there is a general feeling in the ranks and files of the Congress that Gandhi family must remain in the picture.

Secondly, to end the leadership crisis in the Congress, Rahul Gandhi needs to take initiative to challenge the well-organized, ideologically more compact and accompanied with powerful leaders of BJP, as for now he seems to be only the leader within Congress to stand against the BJP, and definitely in the recent time he has being doing so with courage. Still, the Gandhi family have the nationwide reputation as well as recognition which no other leader within Congress has. In nutshell, without an inch of doubt one can firmly accept that Congress is on brink of decline, and mainly because of the leadership crisis that has emerged after Sonia Gandhi's deteriorating health condition. And unfortunately, not a single leader either has capability or is efficient to control the situation, in fact none of the leaders have their reach to the wider section of the Congress workers. Most of them are limited to their constituencies or a region. In these circumstances, a leadership overhaul is as indispensable for the Grand old Party as is the need for a Gandhi face at the helm of affairs.

08

A Beginning of New Politics in the Times of New Economy

Three decades have passed when for the first time India officially advanced on the roads of the New Economy reforms in 1991. Since then, hundreds of writings have been published in favour and against the arguments of the new economy policy. In fact, tug a war between the two different arguments is still acute among the economists, politicians, intelligentsia class, and the common citizens. A section in the society holds the view that these structural reforms aren't just desirable, but are necessary to create a 'New India'; a transparent India, globally competitive India and for innovative India. Further, their arguments extend to better lives for all Indians. Contrary to argument in favor of economy reforms, many politicians, economists and social activists have a very different view, perhaps, they firmly believe that the new economy reforms are chain of slavery for vast Indian masses, and due to the implementation of it, there has been severe rise in the gap between the 'haves and haves not', which is a matter grave concern for all Indians. Perhaps, there are two extreme lines or viewpoints – one goes in favor of the reforms while the other argues about the drawbacks and calls it to be anti-India and anti-people. In fact, new economic reforms also divided the economists in between Right and Left in the worst acute form.

Nevertheless, as we are all aware that it was the Congress who apparently architect the new economic reforms to bring the Indian economy on the track; as they claimed for. Thou, the chapter isn't for the analyses of the economic reforms, but my prime motto is to analyze the politics of economic liberalization in India. It is quite true that liberalization policies initially began to enter into India during the second phase of Mrs. Indira Gandhi's return to power in the 1980s. But the act of Indira didn't raise political opposition, in fact, the major and for the first time, the liberalization policy came to attack when Rajiv Gandhi tried to push it further. Devilal Chowdhary, opposition leader of Haryana evoked the people against the so-called "Modernization" of Rajiv Gandhi during his election campaign in 1987. Certainly, Devilal was able to spread the message in Haryana that Delhi rulers do not have peasant interest at their heart. Gradually, this sipped into the hearts of the poor rural people, especially among the wider section of the Scheduled Caste. But the real kick-off of privatization, liberalization and globalization began in 1991 with an official announcement by the Congress government in the leadership of Narasimha Rao and Dr. Manmohan Singh, finance minister in the government then, and later 2004 to 2014 he also remained the Prime Minister of India. It was the changing time of the Indian economy system of the country, we were on the course to transfer from the Nehru-socialism of mixed economy to open market. As some also call it the neo-capitalism phase of India which centered around privatization. It was a declaration of the shift in stance from a welfare state to monopoly capitalism. It was also the time since independence, when congress was all alone without Gandhi-Nehru members. As Rajiv Gandhi was assassinated, and his wife Mrs. Sonia

Gandhi was not ready to accept any kind of responsibility, only in 1998 she took the charge of Congress by then the water was up to the neck. Only in the second phase that is 2004 to 2014, Mrs. Sonia took some kind of initiative from the onslaught of the reforms when Dr. Manmohan government launched one of the ambitious and much awaited NREGA, to provide job guarantee to the rural unemployed. But by far, the post-reform period witnessed, and still witnessing, a whining of the gap in the rates of growth between the richest and the poorest states in India. The states like Gujarat and Maharashtra resemble Singapore while the states like Bihar, Uttar Pradesh, Orissa etc. seemed to be Sub-Saharan African countries.

Anyway, now the Indian economy is on the track of privatization and monopoly capitalism which is a part of neo-capitalism. The reform that was initiated by the Congress government in 1991 is now toward the rapid speed with more and more shrinking of public sector units and limiting the welfare schemes, as we observe that after the departure of the Congress for two consecutive times, the BJP government in the leadership of Narendra Modi is all set to speed up the pace of the economic reforms; in fact he has started rigorously by selling out the PSUs and cutting the welfare schemes. But here I'm not to judge the impact of economic reform on the Indian economy, but to analyze the impact on politics in the stage of economic reforms.

How Politics and Economy are interwoven – Jeffry Frieden, a professor at Harvard University states, "Politics and Economics are intricately and irretrievably interwoven – politics affects the economy and the economy affects politics." Undoubtedly, this natural approach has been proven in understanding the government and societies; further it can be helpful for those who are interested in changing government and societies. It has become the tool of the modern democracy where politics and economy are integrated into each other. As, we are all aware of the fact that every government has to take decisions on the various aspects such as, What restrictions it has to impose and when to loosen them or where a government is supposed to spend the money and how to raise the money, and what national concerns can be limited to favor international cooperation.

This phenomenon is better acknowledged to us when we peep into Indian politics with the viewpoint of dissecting the difference of economy. Karl Marx rightly said that it is the economy that decides the fate of politics, and not politics. Whatsoever, it is the economy that is the dominant factor which brings changes in the world. This is an important distinction from other major theories in international relations. History of different phases reveals the significance of the economy; from the slavery to Monarchism, and then the capitalism all narrate the story of the nexus within the politics and economy, and indeed economy always played substantial role in deciding the fate of the politics of the time.

Indian political history is no different to other parts of the world. In the post-independent India perhaps, we gone by different phases of economy i.e., we began the journey from the mixed Indian economy to New Economic Policy, Narsimha Rao-Manmohan Singh were the two top bands who officially laid the foundation stone off the New Economic Policy; though unofficial and in a silent mode the policy started enacting itself during the Indira regime of second phase, in fact, Rajiv Gandhi also expanded it, but not officially. Was it the need of hour or the compulsion for the country to go head toward the revolutionary change in the economic structure of structure. Certainly, the story reveals that the 80s was the decade of severe economic crisis that India was facing. There was extreme pressure on the Indian government from the International Monetary Fund (IMF) and World Bank to bring changes in the economic structure of the country with a motive to open the doors of capital flow in and out, beckon with privatization and liberalization policies for free market competition. Earlier, Indira's government was the sandwich between the bipolar politics of the world. Somehow, she was able to resist but no for very long. With the collapse of the Soviet Union; a block of the two, the USA remained an unchallenged block, thereby dictating the economy on its own terms and conditions. Here, India found itself trapped, with no other alternatives then to accommodate with the worldwide changing situation.

But the international situation wasn't only the cause for making substantial changes in the economic structure of India, in fact, the major problems which overtook the Indian economy were primarily the result of certain political imperatives. As more and more sections emerged with demands of state resources. On the contrary to demand governments were increasingly unable either to meet the demands or diffuse the clamor for them. This resulted in the gradual abandoning of fiscal prudence from the mid-1970s. As a result, India's foreign exchange rate fell dramatically at the end of the 1980s. The early years of the 1990s also witnessed the sinking to nearly half. The international situation was also threatening for India, as Iraq invaded Kuwait in 1990, led to a shoot in the price of the Crude oil, as a result the foreign exchange was found to be in an alarming situation. All these factors compelled the Indian government to immediately come over the massive fiscal deterioration, and this could be done in only one way to come out of the gimmick of a mixed economy, which Congress virtually masked for some time.

The 1980s was horrible for India, as the economic growth rate was barely around 5% yearly. The political situation was volatile. Many states of India were amidst of violence – ethnic violence in Assam had torn apart the North-Eastern state, while Punjab was facing the Sikh militancy at its height, which claimed the life of Prime Minister Mrs. Indira Gandhi in 1984. And thereafter, a holocaust was seen on the streets of Delhi and other cities where Sikhs were brutally massacred and treated with hostility for some time. The hope of 1984 soon lost with the defeat in the next general election for the Congress and Rajiv Gandhi. Then, there was a political interregnum between 1989 and 1991. It was the time when the Congress party didn't lead the government, it was Janata Dal who formed the government with the support of Right and Left parties. The end of decade also observed the cut throat division of the country on the lines of caste and religion. In order to keep the array of economy intact, the Indian government borrowed heavily from other countries and internally also. Amidst of all disarray on the platform of economy and politics, general elections were called in 1991, and while campaigning for the Congress the former Prime Minister and the son of Mrs. Indira Gandhi was assassinated by Tamil militants in suicidal bomb blast when he was going to address a rally near Coimbatore in Tamil Nadu. Anyway, the result of the elections wasn't in favor of congress nor was against. Though Congress could not gain the absolute majority, it became the largest party in the Lok Sabha, and by the virtue of that Narasimha Rao who elected the leader of the party was called to form the government.

A New Decade with New Politics and Economy – The economic crisis led Narasimha Rao, a non – Nehru-Gandhi Prime Minister of a minority government break away himself from the traditional mindset and attempted an unprecedented, comprehensive change, in fact, the change initiated in India after many years of china changed its course. We aren't going to discuss much about the impact of economic reforms, instead concentrating on political explanations for the reforms. Soon it became realistic that India was on two boats at a time – the economic reforms and the Hindu nationalism, and this in fact, continued from there upon to the day. So we observe that the politics of economic reforms was carried on the shoulders of communalism. Is there any relation between the two? Certainly, capitalism sometimes requires crafty communalism to rescue itself from the crisis. It has been seen in the past too; Germany during the Hitler's regime used polarization of society in the name of Christianity and Jewish to save itself from the ongoing economic crisis. Thus, in a sense the change in economic policies and globalization are somewhat responsible for giving rise to reactionary politics too. One political analyst Karat emphasized that globalization breaks down national barriers and erodes the sovereignty as well as autonomy of a country. It is the imperialist powers who sponsor globalization, as it is their agenda to seize the market of other countries; especially developing countries, so that they could regulate the economy and flow of capital, but for this the ruling class need to suppress the movement of people which resist the onslaught of big capital. Here in such cases authoritarian centralized states supported by religious chauvinism protect them from uniting the toiled working class; this we have been observing since 1991, and gradually it is sharpening in the Indian context. The more repressive laws mean more polarization in the name of religion, and therefore India saw major disturbances in 1992-93 because of the Ayodhya crisis, which led to riots in many parts of the country between the Hindus and Muslims. Eventually this outraged saw the trajectory climax in Gujarat; where state sponsored massacre took place against Muslim people.

However, after the implementation of New economic reforms, the Indian economy is said to have an unprecedented growth rate of over 7.5 per cent, which by all means was remarkable performance, especially when we compare the economic situation of India just a few years back. The initial impact was seen in the economic states of people especially in the rural region. The agricultural wages that decreased that dipped by around six per cent, suddenly grew over five per cent per year during 1993-94. Employment rate also shooted to seven million in 1994-95, and inflation rate was under the control to below five percent.

Do we conclude, all was well? In fact, it was an incomplete picture. Though, from the top it seemed that reforms were doing great, and were quite successful. But when it comes to nuances of politics, we would find the picture of political instability, as no single party was able to garner a majority for more than two decades. In fact, there was a large section of political parties and leaders as well as economists' outcry against the economic reforms and charged it to be anti-poor. The other important thing that surfaced in the history of the

Indian economy was the advent of crony capitalism, which really hurt the spirit of competition; in fact, it dismantled sentiments of competition.

Nevertheless, it is equally true that a wider section within Indian society had very little idea about the drawback or significance of economic reforms that was started by the Congress in 1991. In the 1996 general elections, Congress lost, and for the next two it had been a mashup of different political parties coming together to form the government, and then departing. Finally, after the unstable period of two or so years, a next general election took place, but for the Congress that election was Waterloo, as for the first time the right-wing BJP under the leadership of Atal Bihari Vajpayee with the support of some regional parties formed the government at the center. And with this, congress not only disowned Narasimha Rao, but also distanced itself away from the 'legacy' of economic reforms. Mr. Atal Bihari Vajpayee who campaigned on the chariot of "Swadeshi", soon took u turn and argued for rapid economic reforms, and to balance his government set off the agendas of nationalism like Nuclear explosion, Kargil war that eventually brought disregard for him and his government, as unfortunately, we lost several soldiers on the harsh terrain in the Kargil area of Jammu & Kashmir. Not surprisingly, these actions cost him dearly. The slogan and issues that his party rose gradually saw fading. But still something was about to arrive and that took place just before the 2004 general elections his government brought the bill of 'no pension' for government employees. This was the severe attack on the Constitution of India, as the Constitution announces India to be a welfare state, but denouncing the very scheme was showing the mirror to the constitution. Whatever may be the obligation, it is true that Vajpayee led coalition government more rigorously followed the economic reforms agenda of Narasimha – Manmohan Singh government. The following foot to foot in fact, lowered the political temperature and drew many to relook and review the significance of economic changes that was initiated in 1991, but Vajpayee did so with ingredients ethnicity, caste, and religious composition that were sprouting in different parts of the country, especially in the Northern India. But the tangible theory couldn't work for BJP, as it didn't work for Congress earlier; though Vajpayee used that in a more ruthless way compared to Narasimha' s government. Despite all proclaim, 2004 general elections failed to accommodate the theory of India Shining campaign, and as a result Vajpayee government didn't come back to power, but it won't be agreeable to say that BJP completely rooted away. But for sure, this was the first time it looked that political parties were competing with each other over economic performance, and on economic issues. Thou, it took long time (ten years) to return to power, but this time the party regained its feet firmly and undoubtedly with more hostility and strength to take the left-out task of the both, Congress and BJP at speedy pace under leadership of Narendra Modi, and it is still in process.

The Background the political Context of Economic Reforms – The coalition ventured on the political landscape of India from 1989 to 2014, where almost all the major parties were in alliance to one or other regional and smaller parties. In fact, for more than the two decades, the Indian politics was divided on the broad three platform; United Progressive Alliance (UPA) led by Congress, National Democratic Alliance (NDA) led by BJP and lastly but was effective during the first decade of the new millennium was the left front which was by CPI(M). In the beginning, the coalition was seen only in national politics, but gradually it firmly took the place in state politics too. But nevertheless, the politics was chaotic and rhetoric, and wider society was fractured along the lines of ethnicity, linguistic, caste and religions. Despite the factious tendency in the political arena, there remained a comprehensive continuity in economic policies and thrust for reforms.

While retrospecting, it has been observed that the politicians were forced to go with the policies that determined some kind of improvement in the economic lives of the people; in nutshell economic performance was only criteria left for the politicians for their political survival. That is why, throughout the first decade of the 21st century and later also, in addition to the innovative social agendas, most of the political leaders also promised to deliver higher economic growth. The one thing was certain that economic growth was now the agenda of the people, and therefore no party could or can escape from it, something very unique and peculiar, as it wasn't heard in India before the 1990s. In fact, no election was fought or won on the issue of development (Vikas) and on the promises of economic growth. This was a radical change that Indian politics witnessed in the last couple or more decades. And for this we can appreciate the policy of economic reforms, despite standing and arguing against the new economic policy.

Now we are in a different era of Indian history, we have surpassed the period of state-driven economic self-reliance, and have entered into an economy of private sector promotion and competitiveness, which poses a threat because it reflects the interest of industrialists, big farmers and bureaucrats. What liberalization really refers to – indeed it is a set of policy measures aimed at loosening governmental control on the functioning of the private economy. And that is why where this policy has friends, contrary to supporters, in large scale there were people who opposed the policy, and among them the most important ones were the rank and file of Congress. Apart from them the members and leaders of left parties and socialists, and many rural groups also opposed the economic reforms, as some of them have a view of point that it is surrender to the international capital or imperialism or the IMF and World bank dictated policies.

Certainly, it is the only side of the coin that is reflected in the argument of those who are against such reforms. They build castles of illusion, definitely there are dangers, but how much and what are obligations, one requires to analyze. Certainly, the economic reforms or liberalization didn't mean a change of goals set in 1947, indeed the goal was very clear then like industrialization, self-reliance India, reducing poverty etc. the new economic reforms can also serve in that direction; only the thing that requires is to have cautious approach with vigilant eye. To a large extent, Congress did it during 2004 to 2014, while in the government. It was the time when Congress confirmed that economic reforms continue along with the welfare schemes, so that common people need fulfilled. But later in the years, we witnessed a drastic change in the policy, and now eventually all the major PSUs are either sold out or are waiting for their turn to be grabbed by MNCs.

As we know there are two sides of the coin, so economic reforms have negative as well as positive impacts. Contrary to its negative impact, we also see flourishing of infrastructure in the course of the two decades. A massive infrastructure build-out is lowering costs: railways, rural electrification, national highways, rural roads, housing and air connectivity. The growth in infrastructure made the life of people easier as well as cut the cost and time. Traveling by air was a dream for an ordinary Indian in the last century, but now it has reached to ease the life of a common Indian. In nutshell, the structural reforms unleashed by the Congress from 2004 to 2014, balanced a better life for the larger section of Indians by mingling the two economies – the mixed economy and the economy of privatization, liberalization, and globalization.

However, it would not be right to reach the conclusion that the earlier 'Nehruvian' strategy was wrong. Indeed, it is of historical significance. It provided the base for the Indian economy to a certain depth, and eventually increased its bargaining power as well as its independence. But over time some negative features also accompanied and developed with it. Further, the response of the world with the changes played a pivotal role in shifting the strategy to achieve the same goal with rapid growth. Today, when Congress implemented the new economic policy along with the Nehruvian idea of building the nation, it definitely bore the fruit of success and growth for the Indian economy, as well as made the life of Indians much better. The slogans like 'Garibi Hatao' (Remove Poverty) transited to the reality of new India.

Today, Indian economic reforms and politics are collateral, as both strengthen one another. It has been witnessed that political competition creates the conditions to improve economic growth. Since the declaration of economic reforms by Narasimha Rao's government to Manmohan Singh's second tenure in 2014, there had been coalition politics, and if I'm not wrong then coalition politics requires more democratic negotiations, and under very different circumstances they are able to reform the economy in a better way. This view is in contrast to the popular belief that economic decisions can only be taken by a strong political leader, with a stable legislative majority. This suggests that when political competition is high, the growth rate tends to move higher. Nevertheless, it is needless to point out that the economy is a web of complexity. But, if the political competition is stabilized then it is possible for the economy to move into a higher gear, and that we observed over the years while investigating and analyzing the Indian economic growth.

The bottom line is – Markets function and thereby, participants flourish when trade is open and competition is intense, but when monopoly erodes the competition, and captivate the market and enthrall the rights of others over the market, this eventually disrupts the efficiency of the market. The same narrative is equally true in the Indian political sphere also. Whatever you urge for, but certainly we can firmly stand and believe that political dominance in no way is an assurance for economic reforms, the present political scenario is the testimony of the statement. As one acknowledges that despite the big majority, the economy is in flux, with no real prediction for the future. In fact, again and again it has been observed in several countries, including India that political dominance can create an overburdening of economic reforms which may turn it redundant.

Finally, we can say that there have been two different phases of economic reforms. In the first phase from 1991 to 2014, it was the politics that controlled the economy, whereas, after 2014, now it is the high time when politics is controlled and challenged by the economy. The second phase is at the mercy of crony capitalism, entirely subjugated. Surely, politics needs to be overcome, and this could take place only when the economy of the country is dealt with by the Indian parliament, and not in the chambers of corporate houses.

09

Organizational and Structural Crisis within Congress: Tearing the Hope Apart

Political parties are......voluntary groups, some are more organized, some less, which claim in the name of a certain idea of the common interest and of society to assume, alone or in coalition, the functions of government.

– Raymond Aron

Indeed, political parties all over the world play a dynamic role in the system, as they are the ones who are either responsible or representative governments. They aren't just dominant, but also creative and comprehensive. The Party is the political force that has emerged to make democracy workable in its indirect form. It serves as the foundation of representative democracy and perform all major institutional and functional activities i.e., contesting elections, forming government, formulating opinion of the electors, taking major decisions when their own party is ruling etc. it is the party that formulates the policies and programs of government and implements them in furtherance of its objectives. In other words, parties are inseparable to modern politics, they are the first and last choice of democracy.

A modern political party usually comprises three components – organization, structure and ideology. Here, we shall discuss the two essential components i.e., the organization and structure. As political parties have been dominant agents in political life of the last century. No other institution attracts as much public interest and public disapproval as do the activities of political parties and their leaders. Nevertheless, parties provide the organization for mobilization and participation and the symbols and ideologies for political identification and articulation. However, it has been observed again and again that democratic political system sustains itself not merely by the ideological structure of the party, but mainly by the commitment of the parties to values, the rules of game and norms that a system envisages.

India observed the democratic value very late compared to the European countries and the USA, but showed valiant efforts once it became free from the clutches of British Colonial rule. The frontline party of the national movement, the Congress consolidated organizationally and gained legitimacy with the government and the people; due to which a political process for political parties and politics gained the environment to set the thing into motion. Gradually, nationalist sentiments and mobilizing the masses in the post-independence period began, and consequently, political beliefs and political culture also gained momentum in the socially, economically and politically diverse India.

The Early Organization and Structure of the Congress – There is no doubt that political organization and competition began among the parties and within the party since independence. This tug-a-war was around the structure of political authority in the larger political system and in fact within the party organization., and Congress was the forerunner being the largest and established party. The other parties like CPI, Socialist etc. were organizationally as well as structurally too feeble in comparison to the giant and the oldest party of India, Congress.

Congress finds itself in crisis – There are two occasions when Congress party and its leadership found itself in deep crisis. firstly, it critically phase began during the end of the 1960s and remind almost although the 70s, when Congress for the first time found itself torn out between the two camps which finally ended up in the split of the party, whereas, 1977, just after the emergency, the party under the leadership of Mrs. Indira Gandhi received a crushing defeat, when Mrs. herself lost her own seat. But soon the crushing defrays turned into victory when Congress regained the power and thereby ruled for the next five glossy years in the leadership of Mrs. Indira, and later after the assassination of Mrs. Gandhi, her son Rajiv Gandhi continued into the office for next five years. Then, for a span of a little more than two years, the Congress remained out of power but then again formed its government in the Centre. Thereafter, consecutive defeat was foreseen – first in 1996 and thereafter in 1999. But when no one thought of the victory of the Congress, it leaped back to power in 2004, and thereby continued in power for two terms; 2004-2009 and 2009-2014. The 2014 elections were the real and disastrous setback for the Congress, in fact, it was the most dismal performance of the Congress in the history of electoral politics; just able to achieve success in just forty-four seats and at the state level the Congress continued to witness severe and unexpected defeats one after another. The next general election also remained disastrous for the Congress. At both occasions the BJP in the leadership Narendra Modi was able to clinch fabulous victory, and brought a debacle rout for the Congress. For the first time, the Congress looked to be very feeble in terms of organizational and structural forms, and for the first time in the history it was seen that Congress doesn't really know what it actually wants and where it stands. The organization of the Congress seems to be scattered and leadership lost its command on the rank and files. The inner conflict emerged acutely, and it brought split in the party again and again. Before going into analysis about the problem that Congress is facing presently in its organization and structure let's have a glimpse of its organizational structure.

An Overview of the Congress Organizational structure – Since the independence of India, Congress as a party has played a crucial part in the Indian politics, in fact, it has tributed a lot in making the Indian constitution of India, and undoubtedly been a main party in waging struggle against the British colonial rule, and ultimate by its resistive efforts able to bring an end of the Union Jack from India. But as everyone is aware that a political party can achieve its goal only when it has compact and strong party structure and organizational strength, and definitely the Congress has been blessed by both for a longer time after independence. It was only later in the years, the debacles in the party became evitable. How and when it degraded and slipped from its position that we shall discuss in the later part of this chapter. Right now, to understand the organizational structure we shall focus upon its organizational structure:

1   At National Level: The President.
2   The Working Committee.
3   All-India Congress Committee.
4   The Parliamentary Board.
5   The Central Election Committee.
6   The Congress Session.

The National President: The National President is the highest office of the party. The president of the national body is the highest office in the Congress. The president is head of the AICC. All the major decisions are taken in the working committee along with the president. The working committee consists of the President of the Congress party, the leader of the Congress Party in Parliament and twenty-three other members of whom twelve are elected by AICC, and the rest are appointed by the President. The president appoints a treasurer and one or more General Secretaries from amongst the members of the Working Committee. The President has the power to appoint one or more secretaries/joint secretaries from elected members of AICC. The Working Committee is the highest sixty-six executive authority of the Congress and has the power to carry out the policies and programs laid by the Congress and AICC. The members of AICC meet twice a year. It has the power to frame rules in tune with the Constitution and implement the programme of the work as laid down by the Congress. It is a working committee that elects a Parliamentary Board which is composed of the President and nine other members including the leader of the Congress Party in Parliament. The Congress President acts as the chairman for the purpose of regulating and coordinating the Parliamentary activities of the Legislative Congress Parties and also frames rules on that behalf.

The other committee is the Central Election Committee which is consist of members of Parliamentary Board and nine other members for the purpose of making selection of the candidates of the state and Central legislature and conduct election campaigns.it is the committee that frames essential rules to guide the Pradesh Election Committee with regard to selection of candidates and other matter related to the conduct of election. Congress also holds Plenary Congress Session (PCC) once in three years. The President of Congress and all other delegates are part of it. It forms a Reception Committee which works under its general guidance. The Congress Session considers resolutions recommended by the Subjects Committee. If either AICC or majority of PCCs decide. Then at the state level, the Congress has the following organs-

1 The State Congress Committee called the Pradesh Congress Committee (PCC).
2 State Working (Executive) Committee and State Parliamentary Board.

Most of the features at the state-level in the Congress party are similar to the All India level. It is the supreme party organ in the state to guide and direct the activities of the lower organs of the organization. Gandhi was of the vision to give Congress a broad-based organization. He established district units at the district levels to develop Congress mass base. Indeed, the district party structure always occupies a very strategic position in the hierarchy of the party organization. It plays a decisive role both in the nomination of candidates and in transmission of policy decisions from higher echelons to lower ones.

Lastly, but perhaps the most significant are the primary structure of various organizations of the party ie., the village committee, Area committee, Mohalla committee etc. These structures had been the eyes and ears of the Congress that brought all kinds of information for the party, and probably helped the higher authorities in framing the policies and programs according to the demands of the people. This structure proved to be very supportive for the frontal organization of the party as well as to the party itself. As Congress is able to expand its ground in every section of the people ie., women, workers, employees, students etc. by the virtue of their frontal organization and its devoted cadres and leaders.

It won't be justified if we don't recognize the frontal organization, and their role in expanding the mass base for the congress. Let's go with the glimpses of congress frontal organization who continue to play pivotal roles in building the Congress party again and again. In fact, these organizations not only built up the party, but also helped in raising the voices of the people over and over and again. These organizations also acted as the opinion creator and also the feedback provided by the frontal organization helped the Congress party in knitting the policies and programs of the party into bits and pieces.

Some Frontal Organizations – Over the years, the Indian National Congress has served its purpose through various organizations that continuously are part of the Congress in one way or the other. Some of the many that work in the different sections of Indian society is – Mahila Congress, Youth Congress, Seva Dal, and National Students' Union of India (NSUI). Each Frontal Organization has its own Constitution as well as membership other than the members of the Congress Party. In fact, there are other organizations like Indian National Trade Union (INTUC) which aren't concerned to be a frontal organization of the Congress, but it is regardless to say that such organizations show their beliefs and faith in the ideology of the Congress.

Thus, on papers and in the theoretical world Congress Party is as strong and build up a party as iron. But, does it really give a fitting reply when it comes to the reality of the world? Definitely, the question in itself troublesome for the Congress and its leaders, and many times it has been observed that the leadership eyewashes such questions, as it makes them stand at the square. Let's analyze the organizational and structural condition for the last five decades, and try to find the circumstances of how the organization drastically fell apart.

Era of Mrs. Indira Gandhi and Congress's Organization – Indeed, in the wake of the Congress' defeat in consecutive general elections and remaining out of power in both the Central as well as many states, there is perhaps, an essential need to probe the reasons for party's dismal performance, and the one reason that immediately strike to mind is the torn-out condition of the Congress's organization; Party as well as frontal organization which once been the solid pillar of Congress glory. It was the time when Congress took the challenge to build its organizational structure everywhere ie., from the village to towns and cities to solidify the forts. It was the time when the leaders of the Congress weren't just leaders but in fact, they were the service provided (Sewak) who continuously worked for the betterment of the society. In nutshell, there was a time within Congress when it was known for its culture of devotion and sacrifices, and not mere portfolio holders. The early leaders like Mahatma Gandhi, Jawaharlal Nehru, Sardar Patel and others developed and trained the Congressmen as ideological and political cadres and not mere the observer or the blind devotees of Congress and its leaders. Such cadres still when Congress find itself in a murky position, they are the one who are standing firmly behind the Congress, without any lust of power. In short – a real Congressmen; equipped with Gandhian ideology and principles of Congress. Such rank and files of the Congress were the palanquin bearers of the Congress.

But unfortunately, later in the years especially in the 1970s and onward there was negligence toward carving leaders at different levels. It was the time when Congress was heavily centralized in its decision making, the Congress has a top-down style and heavily dependent on the Nehru-Gandhi family to provide it with leadership as well as votes to win elections. In fact, at the state level, the party's central leadership had to groom leaders with a popular base who could galvanize the state units of the party. The trend of individual worshiping the leaders became the mark of getting tickets and portfolio in the party, and the criteria of hard work and organizers had very little to do. In fact, for holding the supreme power in the Congress, Mrs. Indira Gandhi damaged the spirit of the Congress which was against the ethics of Gandhi and Nehru to make the party and its ideology, a mass base and not a leader base. Instead, now Mrs. Indira Gandhi became the icon of the Congress, while the ideology was diminished somewhere behind the fame of only one.

This led toward weakening of the organization, though it was slow, but was steady, and impact was seen later in the years, as thereafter mainly the leaders focused on individual leaders, and primarily not concerned much toward solidifying the organizational structure at the grassroot level. As a result, it was the period when Congress went through several splits and egos of the leader that ruined the party structure to some extent. Even the crushing defeat of Congress in 1977 didn't give any lesson to Congress, rather inner conflict of Janata Party brought them down in less than three years, and people had no other option but to bring back the Congress into power. So, we can say that Congress came back to power in 1980 due to their own ability, but more because of the non-governance of the Janata Party. But the dent had already started to take shape in weakening the organization in the years to follow. This phenomenon can be understood further with an example that organizational weakening and demand of icon figures that are members of the Nehru-Gandhi family grew simultaneously one after another or hand in hand. The Party started assembling around the loyalists of the Nehru-Gandhi family, and avoided the two-line struggle and debate within the party's rank and file of the Congress. As a result, it continued to be out of power again and again.

The New Millennium and Congress lost Substantial Ground – Thou, still after the two disastrous elections and consecutive defeats has shrunk its base in terms of the vote percentage as well as the parliamentary seats, still Congress imagines itself as a de facto alternative to the BJP. There is a reason for such imagination, but at the same time there also need for the Congress to come out with an alternative. And not only in terms of the practice, but requires significant work in organizing the people around its ideology, program and policies. In fact, congress still holds around twenty percent vote shares at the national level, and is also recognized in all over India. However, despite her identity, something seems to be missing and no doubt this is grave matter that the Congress really needs to not only think about, but require to come out and rebuild the organization at the grassroot to give any sought of challenge to BJP (who definitely has a well-defined and knitted organizations in all section of the society) into the electoral politics.

In a recent Chintan Shivar of the party, the former president of the Congress Rahul Gandhi pointed out about the dismal condition of the party and said that the party gradually is losing contact with the people. This was an honest self-reflection at an organizational level by leaders like Rahul Gandhi who still hold strong positions in the Congress. It doesn't mean that it isn't only a crisis in the party, yes Congress, in fact, there are other problems for the disarray in the Congress. But the organizational crisis plays a pivotal role in Congress' shrinking base. Today, Congress as a party that abides with the narrative of the Constitution of India, needs to think of a new narrative. A narrative that will not only counter the BJP-RSS but tune in to the new reality of which we are the part. Indeed, Congress needs to build itself not only for today, but for the future also, and whatever they will sow today, they are going to harvest in the future.

In the present scenario, the Congress party has caught into cross-fire between monolithic Hindu identity and the messiah of unprivileged and minority communities, and finds place at none of the place. As a result, it ends up in a no man's land, and therefore, there is a "loss of connection" with the people and links to a shrinking social base of the party. In the last couple of years or so, India gone through massive movement of minorities especially the Muslim against Citizen Amendment Act (CAA) and massive Farmers Movement, but unfortunately Congress support was only in words, largely it remained out of the scene, in fact, in the case of CAA, the party looked to be reluctant because of fear of anti-Hindu. As a result, once again congress failed to garner the support of Muslims who gradually shifted their loyalty to other parties.

The organizational structure of the Congress is in dismal condition not only at the bottom or grassroot level, but the instances of absence of organization is also foreseen at other levels of the party in recent years. Many of the organization posts are vacant at the state and Central level of the congress organizations. Several organizations are either not active or seeking leadership to run. But this does not mean that revival of the frontal organization isn't foreseen, definitely there is hope, but it lies over how the Congress reacts to it. Rahul Gandhi's concern for the strong organization is a sign of hope for the Congress, but this word relishes around how fast the Congress changes itself and works for building organization.

There isn't a minute doubt that the Congress dominated the larger part of India's post-independence politics, ruled for fifty-four years of the past seventy-five years, either of its own or as the leader of coalition governments. And it could only do basically through a strong organizational structure from top to bottom. Unfortunately, gradually this strong organizational structure fractured with the time; especially the shrinking of the organization began from the era of Mrs. Indira Gandhi when individuals were given more weightage than the organization. Subsequently, a new phenomenon drifted the Congress into its shell preaching the politics of individuals. This new articulation hollowed the structure of the Congress organization, and slowly but gradually the termite of hollowness brought the organization on the brink in several years. Today in many of the states, the Congress is shrunken to an unprecedented level, though there are people who believe in the politics of the Congress, and even vote for it. But because of a lack of organization structure, the Congress isn't able to make its reach among the new voters nor are they able to muster the support of youth. Thus, the new generation is drifting in the folds of BJP which now become the challenge for the Congress to divert a large-scale youth and new voters into the shell of the Congress and its frontal organizations.

As a opposition party and Grand old Party, Congress requires to play dual role – it has set up it organization and at the same time needs to spread its politics in the broad masses, but due to organizational crisis it failed to bring to audience the failures of BJP like – soaring rise in the prices of essential commodities, agrarian crisis that stunned even the ruling government with massive movement, religious intolerance and anti-minority violence in the last eight years or so. In fact, the things even that are initiated by the Congress or its leaders, didn't make much impact on the voters, because of weak organization. In the last few Congresses has not even been able to make proper attempts to systematically criticize the BJP, instead more often to be playing in the ground where BJP likes them to play neither able to venture mass mobilization on any of the anti-people agendas on a wide-scale. Such a political move would have been significant for the Congress for its political and rejuvenation.

The bottom line is – before going to all these, the congress needs to set its own house in order. And for it, the party requires to set in motion a genuine process of democratization, of the party, overhauling of the structure and functioning of the organization is the foremost need of the Congress. The road of success for the Congress goes through rebuilding of the organization and its structures. This requires proper and regular elections for all the posts of the party, deputing people to work in rebuilding the organizations, and finally as well as importantly, Congress needs to respect the cadres and pave the way to groom them as leader of the Congress, and not merely a loyalist of the leaders. Right now, where the Congress stands, it is a jerky position, and therefore it can move any way depending how it acts. The radical reforms that the chapter discuss about will definitely take the Congress toward success, but if it fails to do so, then without reluctancy, I would say that it will only sink further into political oblivion.

10

The Cocktail of Old Strategy and New Politics

We slowly but definitely inching toward the prime question, why Congress lost the election? The answer cannot be in black and white, as politics in itself cannot be imagined in black and white; it has multi-layered colours, and some of them we tried to discuss and drew the readers to some kind of conclusion. Of course, we discussed the dimensions of corruption, dynastic succession and its impact on overall Indian politics and particularly in the case of the Congress, even dissected the economic reforms and its impact on politics and so on. Finally, overhauling these all different issues, we ended on the road to investigate the reasons for the debacles of Congress, but there are some other issues that need a thorough discussion and a light that brings back the legacy of the past time Congress. According to this view point, one more crucial stoppage is there to find the reason for the pathetic condition that for now has been facing.

Today, the Congress as a party needs to invent new ideas, and for it, the party required a troop of young and dynamic leaders on all the layers of the party. But then, Congress finds itself in a strange land of to and fro struggle between the old and new. Does it not sound astonishing to hear about a party that has its legacy from colonial India to Postcolonial or Independent India. After all, without a second thought the Congress ran almost in parallel with the history of India, just forgetting about the recent phase. Leaders of Congress were the leaders of India, and obviously its existence was seen effectively in large part of freedom movement, and duly thanks of it, the party able to garner the title of 'Grand Old Party', which commemorated the party not just a political party, but an umbrella organization where different schools of thought used to co-exist together.

A political order is bigger than any party, coalition, or social movement. Indeed, politics cannot be sustained in a vacuum. Certainly, Congress is trapped in its own problems, as for now it doesn't seem to be a viable opposition party nor a winning proposition. But this hasn't been the first time for the Congress, such a crisis has been faced again and again by this party; 1969, 1977, 1989, and 1996 to 2004 were the period when Congress faced political and organizational crushes. However, it is equally true that every time, the Congress and its leadership gave a crushing defeat to such a drawback, and returned to power in a more powerful and astonishing way. But 2014 and then 2019 was unprecedented, as the situation changed drastically with the massive win of BJP in the consecutive elections both at the central and state levels. In fact, BJP's success is miraculous in terms of seats as well as percentage of margin.

The Major Problem within Congress – It has been a long time when the Congress is confronting its most serious crisis in its electoral history since the first electoral vote which took place way back in 1951. The Congress witnessed consecutive debacle since 2014 Lok Sabha elections, 2019 brought the second defeat in a row. The party has shrunk to the least total from 400 plus MPs inn Lok Sabha in 1984, currently the Congress parliamentarians, including the Rajya Sabha members also, is the tally reaches to eighty-four out of seven hundred ninety-three, while at the state legislative assembly the total tally is just limited six hundred ninety-five. This statistic makes the condition worse for the Congress.

Indeed, for any political party to thrive in a condition that is as hostile as the Indian political climate, the presence of a strong, astute leader capable enough to tackle dynamic political conditions is very critical. The Congress needs to rethink its plan and vision both to modify itself as a party who is looking to come back into power. Undoubtedly, still the Congress is the second largest party in terms of the percentage of the votes that it continues to receive and secondly, it has recognition as well as mass base support in all the nook-n-corner of the country. Apart, the party is also acclaimed to have leadership potential from the top to bottom, though presently it looks to be in a fragile situation, yet the congress cannot be said over and out from the Indian political arena. Indeed, it is still strong enough to hold itself in Indian politics.

But then, a very legitimate question arises whether Indian National Congress is strong enough to take the challenge of the BJP who in the recent years has taken substantial lead over its opponent; ideologically as well as organizationally both. In fact, the question isn't limited only to organizational structure, but it wants more than that. definitely, the BJP has overshadowed the Congress in terms of seeing India and its population in a new way. Definitely, today's Indian isn't like the India of fifty years back nor the voters' demands are as same as was in the early stages of India after independence, a lot of things have changed with the time. In fact, Congress also knows very well that old strategies aren't going to work successfully, but how the strategy is required to be changed; it is the formidable question that brings lines of worry on their forehead. With the emergence of new demands and aspirants, politics has also taken a new shape. Indeed, the new economic reforms have brought tremendous and unexpected changes in the Indian society, the means and mode of production. It is the time a new class emerged in Indian society, which was supposed to be more money-minded and definitely this section of economic growth touched the skyscraper buildings with no time. This section also brought radical changes in the Indian political environment. Money became the functionary of politics, though it played a pivotal role previously, but now it has become more significant. The nexus of politicians and businessmen became the ultimate need of this era.

Though, it is well known to everyone that Congress was the introducer of the new economic reforms, but did the Congress itself was ever ready to transform with the changes, there is little about it? In fact, it seemed that Congress never judged that the changes in the economy would bring significant change in the society. And it happened brutally and with great pace. The attitude of the Indians towards the things changed all of sudden. Contrary to the changes coming in the social order, the Congress followed the old path of challenging its opponent. It continued to go with old-fashioned slogans and policies whereas, by now most of the Indians started following a very different lifestyle. In fact, the new economic policy miraculously intervened in the way one must think and do. The same was understood by the BJP, and therefore able to consolidate and expand its mass support.

While trying to know about the problems of the Congress, it becomes important to understand why the Grand old Party, the Congress, couldn't be able to transform itself with the changes that were shaping at the political, social and cultural levels. whereas, contrary to the Congress, the right-wing fundamentalist party, the BJP quickly changed itself from the party urging 'Swadeshi' to a party of corporate houses. Indeed, they are able to use ingredients of pseudo-religion to garnish the policies like Foreign direct investment, inviting the MNCs, etc. Whereas, Congress sailed on two boats together – they wanted to carry with them the legacy of Nehruvian socialism that is-PSUs and Welfare schemes to continue, and the new economic policies of liberalization, Globalization also to go hand in hand. But inventory and ambitious riding eventually brought the Congress toward disaster.

Other than the aspect of the economic changes, yet there were [are] significant issues that became the last nail in the coffin of the Congress. These issues also need to be introspective.

Gradual loss of Leaders – It was the time in 60s and 70s, when the voters followed the Congress on the name of Nehru or later even on the name of Mrs. Indira Gandhi, but gradually the myth was shattered, and so the loyalty of several also shifted. In fact, after assassination of Mr. Rajiv Gandhi for about seven years, the Congress was led by the people who weren't from the family of Nehru-Gandhi, and they effectively ruled the country for a tenure, and in fact, did implement the New Economic Policies, which itself was a challenge to the old establishment. But this challenge was short-lived. Mrs. Sonia Gandhi was brought into the politics to bring the Congress back on the track, but Sonia by any means wasn't Mrs. Indira, in fact, the hard reality was that the circumstances also drastically changed. Now, Nehru and Gandhi aren't the icons of Indian mass, they want to see a new face who has the potential to generate something unique, in fact, they are looking for charismatic leaders. Here in one sense Indira has her place among the voters, but in the new shape and new ideology – now Narendra Modi is charismatic leaders for the people and against the secularism, and socialist country, the majority of Indians are inspired with Hindutva ie., One nation, One religion and One language, while socialist dream has transformed to capitalist state where the money is valued more than the culture, emotions and brotherhood. Somehow, the Congress party couldn't keep the same image of Indira alive in Sonia nor in Rahul Gandhi. Thus, in terms of potential leadership, still the people are looking for bold and decisive leadership, and unfortunately such leadership isn't seen in the present Congress. This creates a vacuum of leadership in the Congress, however this is filled to some extent by the BJP and its top brass.

The other significant issue that can be related to the old strategy are the tools that are deployed to make things easier in reaching the people. The present scenario isn't the wagon where you can ride on an oxen cart and circulate the information at your desired time. Now, time means a lot to everyone, and that is why use of modern technology is the need of the hour. Here once again the Congress finds itself behind the BJP. Contesting elections has changed in a typical way, now it is subject to management. The parties that work in the light of managing or taking it as an event are found much closer to success. The Congress has taken some steps in this direction, but it is still in a very initial stage compared to the main opponent party. In fact, sometimes it seems to be a dilemma. Definitely, it rattles its position further, and such a scenario has been seen again and again. Even the election strategist Prashant Kishor pointed out that Congress is either hesitant or doesn't trust the data, rather they are more dependent on gauging the party mood through the workers which is old way that Congress continued with in the old days, but for now such method has become worthless, just killing the time and energy. However, much more professionalism is required to groom in the competitiveness era where politics isn't just a good oratory or bringing the voters to the polling booth, but in fact it means more than that. The party needs to keep itself upgraded. Though, the Congress has started initially but still it requires to do much toward it, and further it also requires to come out of the old shield because old customs aren't helpful in the time of politics.

Another major issue that remains a challenge for the party is its repeated failure to establish itself as an ideological counterpoint to the incumbent BJP. While in the Nehru or Indira and to some extent in the period of Rajiv regime, Congress found itself more firmly poised toward its ideology. But in the present scenario, Congress has failed to take an appealing stance on any of the growing issues like unemployment, price rise, slowing of the pace of economic growth etc. Such failure has further shrinked its chances to secure an edge over other parties including the BJP. certainly, for now the Congress cannot be said to be a torchbearer of socialism, though in words its some of the leaders continue to mutters about the Nehruvian era and his socialistic, but in practical world the Congress has gone far away from that and has leaned towards the ideals of economic liberalism and privatization. The lack of firmness of ideology in the Congress has given a major jolt to Indian democracy as a whole, as the voters for now don't have an alternative, and secondly the Congress itself on the roads with nearly 120 elected Congress members shifted to other parties, mainly to BJP from the Congress. Unlike the old Congress, it has often seen in the present time Congress that Congressmen continue to be covetous for power and money, and not much serious toward ideology.

Nevertheless, Congress emerged and consolidated as a challenge to the British force in colonial India. Since then, the Congress has always been a broad national movement than a mere political party. In colonial India as well as in the post-independence period, Congress remained a party that provided a broader platform for people from different social backgrounds. Indeed, nationalism meant something very different for the Congress, there wasn't any sought sectarian approach. Despite the criticism of the party from inside as well as from the other parties, the party never gave its ideology to appease certain communities or groups for the sake of minor benefits. For a long time, the Congress was known for standing firmly on its ideology and keeping the democratic values. But then a time came when the Congress went into shell, and became a party of just the four walls. The adverse impact quickly fell on the Congress, it was the time when Congress declining could be impulse. Since 1984 to 2004, several regional parties with identities of caste, sub-caste, religion make their emergence in Indian politics at a rapid pace. In other words, the fragmentation of power in national politics deepened considerably over the two decades, as result of major social changes the National party, especially the Congress rapidly moved to an era of coalition politics; though this wasn't the new thing. In fact, Congress did this in many states earlier also to ensure their government in states. Who could forget the alliance of the Congress and CPI(M) in West Bengal in 1967. Thus, we can say that it was the revival of the coalition at a larger scale where several parties came together to contest elections as well as to form the government at the Centre and in states.

Shall we call the End of Congress or A New Beginning – After the collateral defeat of the Congress in the 2019 general elections, lot of questions are once started following the Congress, and indeed many of them haunts the Congress itself, as they aren't in the position to answer them all, perhaps it would be better to say that they are right now in a dilemma to come with an appropriate reply. Will the Congress face the same consequences as the Janata Party or Janata Dal gone through or will the Congress revive from their disastrous phase? No one knows the climax of this mystery. But for sure, the things that the Congress is facing in the present scenario, isn't for the first time or isn't humiliating for only the Congress. Perhaps, almost all political parties underwent abysmal situations over and over again. The congress itself faced a major split in 1969, and later in 1978 a minor one, but Congress continued under the efficient leadership of Mrs. Indira Gandhi.

The only party that is the BJP able to avoid such a fate of split, and that too because of the RSS that eventually kept the party and its leaders under its control. Perhaps, the Gandhis played the similar role then of RSS in checking and controlling the egos of the leaders. Though, the party keeps on giving the message that Congress is a grand old party that brought the end of British Raj, but the empathy will not work much. In fact, now Congress needs to think differently; something out of the box, and that has to be done very soon before it gets too late for the Congress.

Indeed, the situation has changed a lot from the era of the Nehru and Indira period of the 1950s to mid 1980s; the Nehru-Gandhi family members, now don't hold the regard, as they had in the earlier period. Neither, the Congress have the influencing slogans like Garibi Hatao Desh Bachao (Remove Poverty) which at a time attracted a massive mass. definitely, we are now living in a very different stage of politics; a stage where society has transformed from bullock cart to automobile. This new generation has very different likes and dislikes. In these years, due to positive government policies, a section of middle class emerged in the society, even a section of scheduled caste and Scheduled tribes consequently emerged and intermingled themselves in the creamy layer of the society because of reservation policies, as well as arrival of the new economic policy also able brought the life of handful people toward the upper strata.

Apparently, the social, cultural and economic lives of the Indian people has undergone the changes, and this change has reflected in the thoughts of the vast section of the people of every section of the community and groups. In this backdrop, a political party like the Congress requires changes. Definitely, no longer, the Congress can carry the burden of old strategy in the new scenario. It is the high time when elections aren't just fought on man power, it requires planning, and management to make ones reach among the audience, and at the same time it has become initial to prepare a mechanism to bring the voters to the polling booth. And this process requires a team of professionals and skilled workers who could continue tirelessly day and night in their work. The BJP has caught the nerve of the people and that is why by now they have become the master of the game, while the other parties including rode on the old wagons, and as a result were still trapped in their shell. Now somewhat, they seem to be coming out of the shell, but reluctantly with 'if and buts'.

What should the Congress do to break the shackles of old times – Definitely, breaking the old habits isn't an easy thing....in fact, sometimes it even can take you toward a danger line. In the case of the Congress, this possibility always remains, but just sitting hand in hand is in no way going to help the Congress. Only it will take the party toward disaster which would be not only horrifying for the Congress and its ideology......but overall it is going to ruin the spirit of democracy.

The Congress as a party definitely should look forward to its revival, but the transformation can take place only by willingness, determination and hard work. The leadership needs to be stronger in their passion and vision, which right now seem to be missing out. It is also important to understand that still the party is crowded with rank and files that are committed to the party and its ideology, and have the zeal to tirelessly work for the party. Definitely, the party has the vision and experience of the senior Congressmen and energy of the young generation who can play a significant role in establishing the party as per the need of the new millennium. But for it, the Congress requires a stability in thoughts and requires respect for the old and the new together without being biased or having a sectarian approach for each other. Many times, it has been observed that the old strategy fits with the new politics when it is intermingled with each other with an approach of success and in a convincing form. Most of the parties around the democratic world are going with strategy of old and new to garner the party and its politics.

Definitely, the Congress party has to work on this with more effort. Indeed, history isn't the thing to forget, but it is a matter to be concerned about and take the experience from it to pave a new way for oneself. Undoubtedly, the Congress is full of such nectar that can make it bloom in the future, but for that the cocktail of old strategy and new politics is a must and ultimate. The positive mindset is going to harvest maximum for the Congress, but contrary to it the negative thought will spoil the party from top to bottom. This we had seen in the past as well. Mrs. Gandhi's bold steps and decisive decisions embarked the party and the leaders to achieve unimaginable success, at the when most of the political analyst were of the view the end of the Congress, she not only rose the Congress to greater height of success, but eventually also the led party to come back in power in 1980.

Finally, I have reached to a point that Congress isn't yet fully shrank to dismal position, in fact, still it has jolly good mass base of over twenty percent despite the organizational weakness, still Congress hold numerous grassroot workers, and still has experienced and energized leaders who turn the things in favor of the Congress. But what really Congress as a party requires is to come together, and avoid the stupidity of stubbornness, as such an act has already damaged the image of the Congress a lot. These follies continue then definitely it will hamper the party image, and will shrink it further. Today, when Congress is going through the worst phase of history in the political arena. It becomes the duty as well as obligation for all kinds of leaders within Congress to jointly put effort to revive the party from bottom to top and top to bottom. As Mrs. Indira Gandhi did in the 1970s and 1980s, and Mrs. Sonia Gandhi did in the last years of the previous millennium and continued to paddle just before the debacle of the Congress.

11

Narrative of Upliftment

"In the game of politics, it is the narrative that is often touted as a powerful predictor of success in politics." The quote is quite applicable in the course of India's current political scenario, especially the way one fashions the narrative, which is equally important as finding a good one. Interestingly, almost all the major parties recognize this fact in the present scenario. In fact, a very newly formed party by Arvind Kejriwal (the Aam Aadmi Party) is able to tighten the nerves of parties like the BJP and particularly the Congress with its narration to influence the voters. And very soon, it made its impact, first in the capital city of India; Delhi, by offering "clean governance." On the basis of this narrative, this party built a strong connection with the people in a really short time. Definitely, Kejriwal's party did the homework very well, and as a result, it was able to flatten its opponents. Second, it seized Punjab's power by dealing a blow to Congress. Although the BJP has very little space left after the "Farmer Agitation" and its strong coalition partner saying goodbye, this has left the party on the square without much hope for the future. Congress definitely had a good chance in Punjab to continue for the next tenure, but the internal fighting and lack of narratives brought the party on its knees.

The Congress has indeed noticed and acknowledged over the years that the party has the potential to lead, but they lack in vision and agenda; in fact, they need a story that they could sell, a narrative that the populace could relate to. It is the time when Congress needs to realize that, in the absence of a compelling narrative, all it has left to do is win. But unfortunately, that alone doesn't qualify one to win the elections, and here the Congress finds itself stuck.

New India Requires New Thinking and Vision: The new millennium put the country on a new wagon wheel, and the old frame couldn't keep up with the new people's landscape. The people demanded new tracks to take the country to a new height. Contrary to the visions of the people, the Congress continues to ride on the old chariot, making poor decisions. Definitely, the Congress party has to understand that today's India is highly aspirational. When comparing today's India to the India of Jawaharlal Nehru, Indira Gandhi, or Rajiv Gandhi, it was a time when India was still recovering from the aftermath of independence. Indeed, those were the times when iconic heroes were the figures that still remain in the minds and hearts of Indians. Definitely, they were a sublime force for the majority of Indians. The stories of valiant, courageous fighters for independence were heard and liked by the spectators. The constitutional legacy was held, and socialism, equality, secularism, and sovereignty were seen with respect and dignity.

Gradually, in the years to come, the Congress couldn't judge the changing mood of the people. Particularly, after 1991, when the Congress itself opened the gates of liberalization, privatization, and globalization. It was the time when the young generation consoled themselves with a new lifeline that narrated a very different story than the older one. They viewed this as a chance to compete on the international market. It was a time when the government prioritized infrastructure development. Urbanization attracted the vast population of rural India, which saw it as an opportunity for their survival because the inheritance rights made their lives pathetic.

The new narratives side-lined the old ones, and finally brought them together in a junk box, only to be heard as fairy tales. However, is that the only factor that kept the Congress enclosed? Not at all, the Congress has its own legacy... ... that had played a significant role and, in fact, even paddled the canoe of the Congress to and fro. What Congress really needs to focus on is building its own narrative rather than calumniating the BJP for its moves, which they have been doing over the years without judging the pulses of the people. Certainly, this will not help the Congress reclaim its former glory.

The Congress is a Grand old party that fought for India's independence, and thereafter brought the country out of the deep seas of trauma, and further took it on the track of development to make India a modern country. However, today, as we see, the party is struggling to survive, all due to its loose ended ideology. As such, it is time to realize and recognize that the core of modern politics lies in an all powerful narrative.

Indeed, India is rapidly changing, so the Congress also has to evolve and adapt to the emerging needs. It is an important time when Congress needs to take a path that deviates from the ordinary. And for this, it should stop following Modi's moves; instead, it needs to venture past the safety of the deadlock.

The Discourse of Narrative changed in the Past too – This is not the first or the last time that Congress has had to develop fresh narratives in response to shifting public sentiment. Congress was forced to break out of its shell on numerous occasions in the past in order to sow the seeds for the party's growth and success. In the post-independence period, Jawaharlal Nehru came up with the inspirational and spiritual slogan "Modern India," which gained massive mass support among all sections of Indian society. Lal Bahadur Shastri continued Nehru's legacy, and Mrs. Indira Gandhi supported and worked for it with a missionary zeal by nationalizing a number of industries to strengthen the Indian economy, create more jobs, and increase wealth for India's coffers so that more programs could be implemented for the oppressed and weaker section of the Indian population; particular emphasis was given to changes in rural India. In fact, it is impossible to ignore the contributions made by Indira Gandhi while she served as prime minister in the 1970s and the early 1980s. She was the first to recognize the political power that the poor yet downtrodden possessed, and she was so viscerally moved by the prevalence of poverty in this nation that she decided to use the 1971 General Election to highlight poverty as the deadliest political weapon while issuing the clarion call of "Garibi Mitao." And the poor were transformed into smiths who held the key to power.

Since that time, every political party has made it a point to include the poor in their platforms and political debates, especially when elections are just around the corner. Definitely, this was the outstanding political achievement of the Congress. This started an unstoppable radical trend, and every political party has since made helping the poor a top priority. In fact, political leaders hail it as a hot cake for eradicating poverty, making it the most sought-after prize in traditional election politics. Since an increasing number of programs and schemes for skilled and unskilled laborers were launched by the government at the state and federal levels over the last fifteen years, India has seen a crucial uprising of an "alphabet soup" of ambitious anti-poverty programs.

It was a time when India's impulses used to beat in rural society, as the majority of people lived and relied on agriculture for survival. But then the decade of the 1990s brought a transformational change in the economic structure with the opening of the Indian economy. The social order in India underwent a wave of profound change as a result of the economy's change as well. The gap between rural and urban life started disappearing. MNREGA, the Congress's visionary project for the unemployed in rural areas, was also developed during this time.

So, the Congress continues to change its discourse in response to societal needs and expectations, which I believe is a good thing for both the Congress and India. This is quite true that politics cannot overcome barriers unless it changes with time and opportunities, and Congress did it admirably for the majority of its political journey in both pre-independence India and post-independence India. It has always been about judging the pulses of the people. In pre-independent India, it played a crucial role for most of the time because every move remained politically correct. On numerous occasions, Congress and its leadership responded with hostility, but at the right time and place to deliver a nail-biting blow to the British; whether it was the non-cooperation movement, the Dandi March, or the Quit India Movement, which eventually became the British government's "Waterloo" on Indian soil.

The Congress shifted from a party fighting for the cause of liberating India from British hegemony to a party prepared to face challenges in a very different role and in a very different situation. Definitely, it took the initiative to develop India in new circumstances and with new zeal and enthusiasm, though there were many challenges, but it downcast those and paved the way amidst all. Indeed, Congress has always remained at the periphery of the narrative, according to the demands and needs of the people and the country. The 50s and 60s of the last century mainly had the narratives of building the country around the periphery of industrialization, as Jawaharlal Nehru had dreamt of a self-reliant and united modern India. "Tryst with Destiny" confirmed his vision of a free India; his entire speech was centered around encouraging the people of India for upliftment and development. He urged his people to come forward and put an end to all social evils such as illiteracy, ignorance, poverty, and so on in order to lead the country toward development.

After the death of Jawaharlal Nehru, his daughter, Mrs. Indira Gandhi, followed the narrative and continued to walk on the principalities that were interwoven by her father and other Congress leaders. Though the jerk had been noticed in between, she and her party faced ruthless defeat, but she and her party managed to return to power after only a couple of years. However, since the party continues to see leaps and bounds now and then, the major jolt came to the party in the form of the emergence of an ideology known as the BJP, which has been spreading since the early 1990s and has now, in three decades, spreads like a fire, engulfing a large section of society.

Though the Congress came back to power, it is true that it continued to shrink in numbers as well as in will. In fact, since 1990, the Congress has formed its government in the center three times, but not a single time it was able to get its own majority, largely continuing to depend on its coalition partners. Finally, the mirage ended when the BJP, led by Narendra Modi, outcast the Congress to its lowest tally of 44 votes. It was an incredible blow for the Congress and its leadership. Thereafter, the Congress was never able to come up with an effective narrative to charge against the BJP. It wasn't just the blow in 2014, but the Congress was also humiliated in the 2019 general elections and lost in the assembly elections to the BJP or its coalition partner. Unfortunately, despite the rising unemployment rate, inflation, etc., Congress couldn't take the opportunity to make such issues a narrative, an agenda, or an issue to firmly raise against the BJP and consolidate itself. Today, it seems as though the Congress has trapped itself in the valley of darkness, where there is no hope and no plan to come out of it. Will things change in the near future? Frankly speaking, I have no idea. But as it is said, in politics, nothing is permanent or mortal. So the same can be said about the present scenario, where the Congress has stuck and, indeed, doesn't foresee its future. It's unfortunate, but equally true, that the Congress is spiraling downward, its energy depleted, and memories of its former glory fading.

In fact, the UPI II blew the gains made by Congress in 2009 with the wind in its sails between 2009 and 2014, when most of its power had boomerang to itself. Due to the fact that it was unable to maintain the narrative that the Congress had previously been able to start. Somehow, it managed to tackle the growing strength of the BJP. The Anna Hazare anti-corruption movement, which specifically targeted the Congress, was successful in gaining support from all spheres of society. Middle-class and civil society members were drawn to the movement, which occupied the Ram Leela Maidan's center stage for several days. Although the RSS and the BJP undoubtedly supported this movement covertly, many progressive segments of society also fell for the Sangh Parivar's trap. On the other hand, members of Congress' lower ranks were hesitant to reach out to such a sizable portion of the populace. The Anna Hazare movement's outcry and the ensuing BJP onslaught, which dealt the Congress one of its most historic defeats and reduced its vote share to under 20%, may have contributed to its current predicament. Without a compelling narrative to counter these events, Congress may have conjured up its current dire situation. In fact, Congress failed to learn from the previous disaster, and as a result, it will not run in the upcoming state assembly elections (leaving few candidates). In addition, Congress expressed outrage in the general elections of 2019 when Narendra Modi returned the saffron to power in Delhi with a sizable majority.

Lesson to Learn for Congress – Following Rajiv Gandhi's murder in 1991, the Congress party was without the Nehru-Gandhi family for almost ten years before finally bringing Sonia to assume the role of Congress president. The early stage of her presidency was excellent for the Congress, as it succeeded in returning to power in many states. This created an atmosphere for the Congress to challenge Atal Bihari Vajpayee government in the center. It was the time when Congress set the narrative, and that really encouraged the entire rank and file of Congress to work together for power. Indeed, the "Mantra" of Sonia worked for the Congress to come back to power after 1996, i.e., nearly after eight years. Despite ten years in power, it once more lost ground. and this time the situation was drastic. It didn't only lose power, but the gravest part was the way it lost despite the many pro-people schemes launched by the Congress party. It was limited to just forty-four members in the Lok Sabha, and its vote percentage fell below twenty percent.

Though the Congress has taken some major steps to consolidate the party, it still needs to rethink. As the party doesn't seem to have a strong leadership or workable structure, its leftist welfare agenda for the poor, which has continued over the years since India's independence, has now been hijacked by the BJP. Though whatever the goal and mission of the BJP, the party is certainly using it to best position itself as the single dominant party in Indian politics. In recent years, they have taken advantage of the free ration for the poor. This really accelerated the support of the BJP among the most deprived sections.

It is true that the Congress party has faced significant challenges in recent years, including a loss of support among voters and struggles to establish a strong leadership and effective structure. The party has a long history in Indian politics, and has traditionally been associated with a leftist welfare agenda that focuses on improving the lives of the poor and disadvantaged. However, in recent years, the Bhartiya Janata Party (BJP) has been able to effectively appeal to these same voter groups and has been able to gain support among the most disadvantaged sections of society through its own pro-poor policies, such as the provision of free rations. This has contributed to the BJP's rise as a dominant force in Indian politics, and has made it difficult for the Congress party to regain its footing. It is important for the Congress party to reassess its strategies and find ways to better connect with voters and effectively promote its policies and vision for the country if it hopes to regain its political influence.

Congress Needs New Narrative, Clear Ideology, Firm Leadership – It is true that political parties in India, and indeed in any country, need to have a clear and compelling narrative in order to be successful. However, it appears that the Congress party in India has struggled to adapt to the country's changing political landscape and, as a result, has been unable to effectively communicate its vision and agenda to the audience. Eventually, this has led to a lack of support for the party and also contributed to its decline in recent years, especially after 2014 onward.

Today, the most important task for the Congress party is to understand the people's deepest needs and concerns in order to craft a narrative that resonates with them. Definitely, to craft such a crafty design requires a deep and intelligent understanding of the issues that the country is facing, as well as a willingness to adapt and change itself according to the mood of the people, to address the issues. Further, the party needs to effectively communicate its message and vision to the people.

Once again, the Congress needs to rewrite its ideological agenda and require it to open the entry gates of the party for people even with rightist views within its broad spectrum of secular politics to counter the BJP surge in the country. But at the same time, the Congress also needs to draw a line to separate itself from the BJP on the issue of Hindutva to give a new vision to its supporters. The same Congress did prior to the 1990s decade, but eventually found itself on the BJP's chariot, particularly during Narasimha's regime. Though Sonia Gandhi's entry into the political arena was able to put a brake on lucrative religious chanting within the party, by then the minority had slipped away from the fold of the Congress.

In addition to building a strong narrative, it is also important for a political party to have strong leadership and a solid organizational structure in order to achieve success. Definitely, the party can revive itself by rebuilding the party organization, repopulating its cadres with foot soldiers and flag bearers at the grassroots level, and setting up realistic goals to achieve a political rebound in the distant future.

The Congress, however, will have to put in a lot of effort in these areas to win back its supporters and regain its former position as a significant political force in India. Finally, I would like to emphasize that it is high time that the Congress look ahead to change its narrative and try to build a new and compelling one that influences the people of India and that people can relate to.

The Congress had steadily lost ground, going from being India's sole dominant party to its pathetic performance in the second decade of the new millennium. It lost several of its bastions, communities, and loyal Congressmen over the years. Despite that, one thing is certain: Congress is still in the political fray, and without an inch of doubt, in the future there is going to be a bitter battle of the two narratives: Congress vs. BJP. Indeed, the Congress has the nation's wide acceptance after the BJP, but what the Congress really needs to ensure is vision, because in politics, decisions play a key role in the party's uprising. And here Congress seems to have lost its ground. Though its narrative is stronger than the BJP's, its agenda is focused on livelihood issues such as unemployment, farmer distress, health, education, and so on, which puts the Congress in a better position. Indeed, it falls short of serving the people's issues or even occasionally playing on the same ground where the BJP appears to be in a comfortable position.

Several things draw us to the conclusion that the victory of the BJP isn't because Indians love Modi's work or vision, or because he is a charismatic leader, or because he is making India free from corruption and terrorism; all of these are baseless and have no reality, but if we count the success of the BJP, it lies in the reluctant approach of the Congress and other opposition to offer a clear-cut narrative. In contrast to the Congress, the BJP is clear about its agenda and mission, even if one disagrees with it, and that is enough for the BJP to maintain power, whereas the Congress has no counter narrative to the BJP. This could be a very strong reason for the decline in support. In order to regain support and win elections, Congress needs to articulate its vision and agenda. And demonstrate its commitment to address the issues that matter most to the people.

The bottom line is that Congress needs to go back and reconsider the consequences that have followed it and are still haunting it. Indeed, the party needs to analyze and introspect why its vote bank has steadily shrunk. Why have communities like Dalits, Muslims, and Sikhs slipped away from the Congress? Though it tried to please everyone, it has now come to a position where there are no takers in Congress, and this happened only in the absence of the positive narration and clear ideology that it upheld in the early stages of post-independence. A party that ruled for over five decades at the center and in almost all the states of the country is currently in an abyss. Certainly, Congress and its leadership have to come up with a solid "mantra" that provides the wings for the party to fly and spread ideas and the vision of the party among the people of India.

It is true that the Congress party has faced significant challenges in recent years, and has lost support in various parts of the country. However, it is important to recognize that the political landscape in India constantly continues to rise and fall, and no party tends to be a permanent loser or successor.

12

Will Mallikarjun Kharge's Presidential Term Be a Rejuvenator for Congress?

Finally, Mrs. Sonia Gandhi decided to resign from her position as party president and Rahul Gandhi who had already clearly shown his intention to not hold the position of the congress President. In fact, Sonia continued as interim President of Congress for nearly two years after Rahul Gandhi opted to resign, and further showed no interest in the post. Thereafter, search for new Congress president began, and finally the historic event of transfer of power was initiated to a leader who was not a Gandhi for the first time in twenty-four years.

Though, the nomination for the post was not less than the drama in itself, where earlier Rajasthan chief minister, Mr. Ashok Gehlot had the blessing of Gandhi family, but sudden rebellious attitude by Ashok Gehlot changed the entire scenario, and Mallikarjun Kharge and Shashi Tharoor became the two contesters of the post. The Gandhi family remained away from the processing, merely to show no Gandhi family interference in the selection of the Congress president. Rahul was busy in Bharat Jodo Yatra, and only casted his vote on the day of voting in Karnataka like other congressmen.

In many ways, the election for the president of Congress can be scaled as an auspicious sign – firstly, after twenty-four years, the Congress was set to choose a non-Gandhi-Nehru president. Secondly, it was the sixth time in the history of the Congress, that Congress was set to have an election for the presidential post. Thirdly, there was shed mark interference of the Gandhi family directly or indirectly.

Now, when we are set to read this book, all of us are aware that the Congress eventually has elected Mr. Mallikarjun Kharge as its new president. It has undoubtedly been a breakthrough for the party, but it is still too early to evaluate and make a choice in light of the upcoming Congress. However, there are some issues that call for some sort of analysis, like how and what will influence the future. But more importantly, most of the Congressmen believe the Gandhis are the only ones who will assuredly not join the BJP, whereas most of the other leaders have either done so or can do so in the future.

The two Congress leaders, Mallikarjun and Shashi Tharoor, competed for the position of Congress president. After all was said and done, Mallikarjun decisively defeated Shashi Tharoor. As told earlier, this time, the family simply came and voted, which I think is a positive sign for Congress. But that does not mean, the Congress is free from difficulties. Given that it is obvious that lasting solutions cannot be found in a day or two, time will tell us what the future of Congress will look like. Nevertheless, for the first time in decades, the Congress saw a direct election with a non-Gandhi president. This election was significant because it was able to send a message to the grass-roots level that those who stay and work for the party would rise from the ranks, which Congress failed to adopt over the years. Another significant impact was that the Congress was able to send a strong message to the village, block, and district-level Congress workers about its intra-party democracy through this election.

A glimpse into the history of a newly elected Congress President – Mallikarjun Kharge, a newly elected Congress president is a veteran leader of Congress from Karnataka. There are few things that we all must know about the newly elected Non-Gandhi-Nehru president of Congress-

- Kharge was born on July 21, 1942 in a poor Dalt family in the Bidar district of Karnataka.
- Later in the years, he became the disciple of Buddhism.
- He lost his mother at the age of seventeen to communal violence, which later in the years shaped his ideology as a secularist.
- Kharge joined Congress in 1969, it was the year when Mrs. Indira Gandhi was expelled from the grand old party.
- Later, at the age of twenty-seven, he became the president of the Kalaburagi town Congress Committee.
- The new Congress president is an arts graduate from government College, Kalaburagi.
- He also got the title of 'Solilada Sardara', which means undefeated chieftain. As he was elected to the Karnataka assembly nine times in a row.
- He also won from the Gulbarga Lok Sabha constituency in 2009 and 2014.
- In 2009, he became the union minister of Railways in the UPA-II government, and also served as Union cabinet Minister for Labour and Employment.
- Kharge was elected to the Rajya Sabha from Karnataka in 2020, and remained the opposition leader in the Upper House ie., Rajaya Sabha, until recently.

- He is the second Dalit president of Congress in five decades after Jagjivan Ram in 1970.
- Two times Member of Parliament from Gulbarga, was defeated by BJP's Umesh Jadhav by a margin of around Ninety-five thousand votes.

Presidential Election: A Historic Move Within Congress – The two consecutive moves by the Congress in 2022 look to become a lifeline for the Congress in the future. Two significant events occurred, one of which we will cover in the next with detail, and the other one which we are sat to discuss about, is related to the Congress presidential election. Although initially the tension was high as the Rajasthan issue reached a boiling point and it appeared that the Congress would suffer yet another blow in a ruled state, somehow, primarily as a result of Sonia Gandhi's intervention, things temporarily calmed down. However, as we all know, the fumes continue to flare out from the ashes. Nevertheless, the presidential election in the Congress party took place in a free and fair manner, where around nine thousand delegates used their voting rights to elect the Congress president after twenty-four years. Undoubtedly, it was a historic event because it was only the second time a non-Nehru-Gandhi president of the Congress was elected and not nominated by any Gandhi family member since Indira Gandhi split the original party in 1969. By all means, this event can be called radical within the Congress and indeed a breakthrough moment for the party, revealing a stirring of change, though it is too early to reach to the conclusion that this event is going to improve the electoral prospects of the Congress at the national level. Indeed, the Gujarat state assembly election didn't bear the fruit of the event, but the Congress was able to form the government in Himachal, whereas in Rajasthan, the tug-of-war between the two stalwart leaders, namely the CM of Rajasthan, Ashok Gehlot, and the young, energetic leader Sachin Pilot, somewhat resolved itself. So, one can say that Mallikarjun Kharge has a mixed record of both success and failure in a short span of time. Nonetheless, there is a widespread belief that the Congress presidency under a non-Gandhi will help in rejuvenating the party and consolidating it into a broad liberal, secular force to take on the BJP and its ideology.

List of non-Gandhi-Nehru Congress Presidents since India's Independence-

Sr. No.	Name of Congress Presidents and Year	Sr. No.	Name of Congress Presidents and Year
1.	J.B. Kripalani (1947)	8.	Jagjivan Ram (1970-71)
2.	Bhogaraju Pattabhi Sitaramayya (1948-49)	9.	Shankar Dayal Sharma (1972-74)
3.	Purushottam Das Tandon (1950)	10.	Devakanta Barua (1975-77)
4.	U.N. Dhebar (1955-59)	11.	Kasu Brahmananda Reddy (1977-78)
5.	Neelam Sanjiva Reddy (1960-63)	12.	P.V. Narasimha Rao (1992-96)
6.	K. Kamaraj (1964-67)	13.	Sitaram Kesari (1996-98)
7.	S. Nijalingappa (1968-69)	14.	Mallikarjun Kharge (2022-onward)

The Gandhi-Nehru family upheld the post several times in the post-independent India. Mr. Jawaharlal Nehru upheld the post in between 1951-55, Indira Gandhi became the president in 1959, 1978 to 1984 respectively. After the assassination of Indira Gandhi, her son Rajiv Gandhi became the Congress president till his assassination. Mrs. Sonia Gandhi replaced Sitaram Kesari 1998, and remained at the helm till 2017, when Rahul Gandhi became president but resigned from the post in 2019, and thereafter, Mrs. Sonia Gandhi returned as interim chief of the Congress.

History of Congress Presidential elections – The grand old party Indian National Congress, which was founded in 1884, had its first presidential election for Congress president way back in 1939 when Mahatma Gandhi backed P. Sitaramayya against the stalwart leader of then, Netaji Subhas Chandra Bose. In the first election Netaji defeated the Mahatma Gandhi backed candidate. Thereafter, the Congress witnessed a second presidential election in 1950, in that election Sardar Vallabhbhai Patel loyalist Purshottam Das Tandon defeated Jawaharlal Nehru's candidate, Acharya Kripalani.

Thereafter, the Congress witnessed another presidential election after say, twenty-seven years, in 1977, when Congress lost in the Lok Sabha election to Janata Party, and thereby, taking the responsibility of the crushing defeat the AICC chief resigned from the post. It was Brahmananda Reddy who defeated Siddhartha Shankar Ray and Karan Singh to become AICC chief. The next election for the post of president was held in 1997 when Sitaram Kesri squared off in a triangular contest with Sharad Pawar and Rajesh Pilot. The last presidential electoral contest, before the latest one, was held in 2000 when for the first and only time Gandhi family was challenged in the election. Jitendra Prasad took on Sonia Gandhi, but he faced a crushing defeat. The latest election of the Congress president was held only last year in which Mallikarjun Kharge overwhelmingly defeated Shashi

Tharoor in a direct contest for the post of Congress President. Which way will the Congress go from here? Will it be a new beginning for the Congress? All these relevant questions will need answers in the future.

The journey of the Congress reveals that Congress had the legacy of electing the president of the Congress whenever more than one candidate contested for the post. Despite the fact that the Gandhi family played a pivotal role, and several times the member of the family held the post, in fact also played a crucial role in the elections where two or more candidates contested election for AICC chief. However, history reveals that on occasions non-Gandhi candidates have emerged victorious; from Mahatma Gandhi's to Nehru's candidates lost the election. This is an inspiring note for internal democracy, where one man or one family, though they have influence, but every time aren't able to change the things according to their wishes. and, here we see the strength of democratic culture amidst Congress.

Will the New President bring new energy and hope for Congress? – Despite the limitation, nevertheless, Congress is able to promote an alternative vision of India through the yatra, while the election of a non-Gandhi president is a surprising event for many. Even the BJP became speechless for a while. In fact, the election has laid to rest the suspicion that the Gandhi's were determined to keep the reins of power in their own hands; further, it was Rahul who reinforced such a vision when he refused to meet any of the Congress Chief Ministers and also denied being part of the selection of candidates for the Gujarat assembly election by saying that it is now Kharge's business to deal with. Unlike Mrs. Indira

Gandhi, in the recent circumstances the Gandhi's gave free hand to deal with things. There are instances when Rahul Gandhi was asked on the matter of the Gujarat assembly elections, but instead giving his own verdict, he requested to ask about it to Mr. Kharge, the president of Congress. Even for his own role in the party, Rahul Gandhi respected the newly elected president who according to him will decide his role.

If we talk about Mallikarjun Kharge, the Congress president, indeed he is a veteran and Dalit leader who hails from Andhra Pradesh. This shift in the Congress party's leadership and decision-making structure can lead the party with more potential toward a more democratic and inclusive approach, as opposed to solely focusing on the Gandhis. Indeed, this has also opened up the possibility for regional leaders to have more influence and input in the decision-making process. However, it remains to be seen how successful this new approach will be in the long run, as well as what kind of benefits Congress will reap from it. In a nutshell, whether Congress challenges the current ruling party or not, all of its hard work will bear fruit, with or without Gandhi at the helm. Both Rahul and Sonia have withdrawn from the leadership, which is a signal and a formal withdrawal from the pyramidal, leader-centered party structure that emerged within Congress with Indira Gandhi, who for the sake of leadership split the party in 1969.

But indeed, the election of a new party president is just one step among many for the Congress party on a path of revival. Gathering resources, building organization, strengthening state and local units, and defining a political line that connects with voters, aren't the task that can be handled by a single individual, perhaps it requires the troop of leaders who tirelessly work for the party. Meanwhile Kharge has the stature and political experience both to play a key role.

Newly elected Congress' President and awaited Challenges – Everything isn't settled or resolved for the new president, rather Congress is in a state of crisis on many fronts. The biggest question that surely may be bringing lines of worry for the newly elected president. Mallikarjun Kharge, is how to resolve multiple problems, and further foresees an opportunity to prove himself in the coming assembly elections and prepare the party for the 2024 Lok Sabha elections. But for now, all eyes are on the Congress top leadership to overhaul internal functioning which is the only way for a possible revival of the Congress as well as India's current political landscape. Indeed, the first and the most crucial task that the new president has in front of him is to save the party from political oblivion.

The advent of a new president of the Congress comes at a time when the party is facing immense political challenges, high-profile exits and defections after a series of electoral losses and intense factionalism in some states. Meanwhile at behest, Mr. Mallikarjun Kharge needs to focus on some of the most critical issues that could hamper the image as well as organizational structure of the Congress, if not resolved as early as possible. Some of those are as follows-

1 Rajasthan leadership tussle – The old rivalry between the chief Minister, Ashok Gehlot of Rajasthan and the young and ambitious leader Sachin pilot is no secret either in Congress or among the people of the nation. This became more strained when Ashok Gehlot revolted against the high command's choice, though later he confessed to his

deeds, but unfortunately the matter hasn't been settled. Right now, the situation looks settled, but the truth lies beyond it, as fumes are present, which can transform into furore at any time. Therefore, it becomes important for the Congress president to settle this problem, especially when Rajasthan is around the clock for assembly elections.

2   Organizational challenges – The biggest problem that the party is severely facing is the challenges with organization. Both senior as well as young leaders continue to leave the party or in conflict with each other. This situation in the party has created hollowness which immediately needs to be brought under control before it gets too late.

3   Building the Party structure in the Hindi Belt – it has been decades since the last Congress had power in the states like Uttar Pradesh and Bihar; the heartland of the Hindi Belt. In fact, these states alone send 120 Lok Sabha seats, and unfortunately Congress share has been negligible. If Congress wants to make any progress in the coming general elections, it has to take the fight to the wall in these two states.

4   Blueprint for 2024 elections – The testimony of Mr. Kharge lies in how he plans for and achieves success in the forthcoming Lok Sabha election which has to be held in 2024. Though, as previously stated, Kharge possesses the stature and political experience to play a key role in reaching out to other Opposition leaders. But here other than that, he also has to ensure a blueprint for the 2024 Lok Sabha elections that places his party in some kind of position against the BJP.

5   Revamping the ideology of the Congress – Another challenge that Kharge has to negotiate with is the ideology

of the Congress. In the last few decades there has been an up and down of the ideology. From Nehruvian socialism, the party shifted to privatization and globalization while often the Congress has taken a pro Hindu stance over the years. In a nutshell, the Congress often tried to play in the court of the BJP and its ideology, without understanding that it cannot beat the BJP in their court. Therefore, Kharge as a congress president has to rediscover the route to crush BJP and its ideology without going into their court.

Further, it appears that under Kharge's leadership, the Congress will move toward a looser coalition whose base will be centered on shared political and economic concerns rather than personalities and charisma. Bharat Jodo Yatra significantly raised the same issue in a larger context, while Rahul continued to talk more about unemployment, poverty, inflation, and the devaluation of the Indian currency but also added the challenges of diversity and unity. After a long time, any Congressman would most likely have ruthlessly attacked the BJP and RSS for vehemently polluting India with hate politics.

Finally, will they be prominent or will they return to the mirror, as is often the case when it comes to the issue of Gandhi? The foremost reply is that the Gandhis are an inalienable part of the party. Perhaps the Gandhi family has given the country three prime ministers, two of whom (Mrs. Indira Gandhi and her son Rajiv Gandhi) were assassinated for the cause of the country. Thus, it is clear that even if the family does not hold any position, the last mile worker draws inspiration from Gandhi's legacy.

The Bharat Jodo Yatra (about which we shall discuss in the next chapter) and Mallikarjun Kharge's election as president—a non-Gandhi—are just two recent instances of the substantial changes the Congress party has undergone. The two recent events give the Congress its lifeblood because they can inspire hope in its members and energize them. Undoubtedly, Mr. Kharge is an experienced and veteran leader of Congress, further, it has been witnessed that he always remains a staunch Gandhian. In the recent past, it has been also noticed that he has been a vocal critic of the Narendra Modi-led government. Such attitude and elevation will definitely give a boost to the cadre.

Secondly, the Congress, in the meantime, will be strongly poised to claim that its internal democracy has no parallel in any other party and that it is the only one to have a central election authority for organizational polls.

Finally, much awaited to watch how the Congress under the leadership of newly elected president, Mallikarjun Kharge pierces the façade of manufactured Hindutva that the BJP and its leader continue to cling to in order to seize or hold onto power since 2014. If the Congress makes the effort with good sense and approaches the democratic struggle with more potential and vigor, it can undoubtedly get back on track. Finally, I would end by assimilating that the election of president and appointment of new non-Gandhi Congress president has taken place at the right time, when on one side Rahul Gandhi's, Bharat Jodo Yatra's success has shown that there is still space left in the country for an inclusive and rights-based form of politics that the Congress represents and can tap into. The only thing that Congress needs is to project its ideological position more clearly and consistently to take on the BJP and also to find ways of tackling institutionalized inequities and inequalities, which have grown on a wider scale in the last few years. And for this, the task is on the shoulders of the Congress president to take out the party from the brink of collapse. Nevertheless, Mallikarjun's experience, and potentiality gives hope and energies to its members. During his presidential term, there is substantial hope of the rejuvenation of the party. The resounding victory in Himachal Pradesh Assembly Elections 2022, Karnataka and Telangana Assembly Elections 2023 and getting greater number of votes than BJP in Rajasthan, Madhya Pradesh and Chhattisgarh could be seen as a new beginning.

13

The Bharat Jodo Yatra

The book unravels the various aspects of the Congress since its formation. Particularly after 2014, the Congress experienced significant organizational and structural setbacks. The book places us in the middle of a sizable tent of ideologies and convictions of one of the oldest political parties in the history of the world, the Congress, which spearheaded a massive mass movement for freedom against the colonial regime and also established the framework for a democratic, secular party in the nation, which is unquestionably currently in serious crisis. In actuality, the BJP has not only overwhelmingly defeated the Congress in subsequent elections after 2014, but it has also worked to undermine the principles that the party has continued to stand for over the years. Today, it appears that the Congress has forgotten the essential components of its political mobilization tactics. However, the Congress suffered serious harm, particularly during the 2019 elections. Even several prominent leaders of the Congress quitted the party in search of better opportunities, and several of them presently seen with the BJP.

But the issue isn't just related to the Congress party alone; in fact, most of the social democratic parties across the globe are facing the same crisis. In India, the widespread adoption of right-wing ideology and neoliberal policies has significantly concealed economic disparities, making it challenging for the opposition to politically mobilize the populace. The Congress, a centrist party, is no exception.

Finally, the Congress decided to mobilize and make its reach out to the general masses through the massive and ambitious "Bharat Jodo Yatra", which intended to cover approximately 3500 kilometres and encompassing twelve states from Kanyakumari to Kashmir. This adventurous and ambitious program initiated by the Congress at the time when the party is going through severe organizational, structural, and ideological crisis or hollowness. This is not first time that such Marches or Yatra is organized in India by any political leaders. In fact, pre-independent India also witnessed such yatras against the onslaught of British. Indeed, who could forget the memorable 'Dandi March' led by Mahatma Gandhi against the salt tax that was imposed by the British Government on Indian people. In fact, the same Dandi March became the semblance of inspiration for Bharat Jodo Yatra. Certainly, Congress' Bharat Jodo Yatra is a political buzz.

To begin, the Congress and Rahul Gandhi waved the flag of the yatra on September 07, 2022 from the last coastal land of south, Kanyakumari; a city of Tamil Nadu, and is scheduled to cover as many as fourteen states – Tamil Nadu, Kerala, Karnataka, Andhra Pradesh and Telangana, Maharashtra, Madhya Pradesh, Rajasthan, Haryana, then the Capital city of India, Delhi, Uttar Pradesh, Punjab, Himachal Pradesh and finally ending the Yatra on January 30, 2023 in Jammu & Kashmir. For this yatra, around 150 days were scheduled for its completion, with a break of a weak from 27 December to 2nd of January, vacation of a weak after reaching Delhi.

Again, on the 3rd of January, 2023, the yatra began its steady journey to go ahead and entered into western Uttar Pradesh (touching only three districts), but against all speculations, the Yatra received a warm welcome in the Jat dominated region of the state. Rashtriya Lok Dal, chief Mr. Jayant Singh extend his hand in support of this yatra, the farmer leader of Bhartiya Kisan Union extended his support while becoming the part of the yatra. Other then, the party just lying at the edge of the death found oxygen when thousands of its cadres from all corners of the states came to be part of the yatra. Thereafter the journey entered into Haryana and from there travelled to Punjab, Himachal Pradesh, finally entered into Jammu & Kashmir.

The Congress did plan its objectives and aim-

1   The aim of the Congress was to raise issues of growing economic disparities and social harmony.
2   The motive of the Yatra was to fight against communalism, unemployment, hatred, inflation and political centralization.

The congress made sure the participant should belong to different background like – politicians, citizens of the country, civil society organizations and political activists.

Route of Bharat Jodo Yatra from Kanyakumari to Jammu & Kashmir

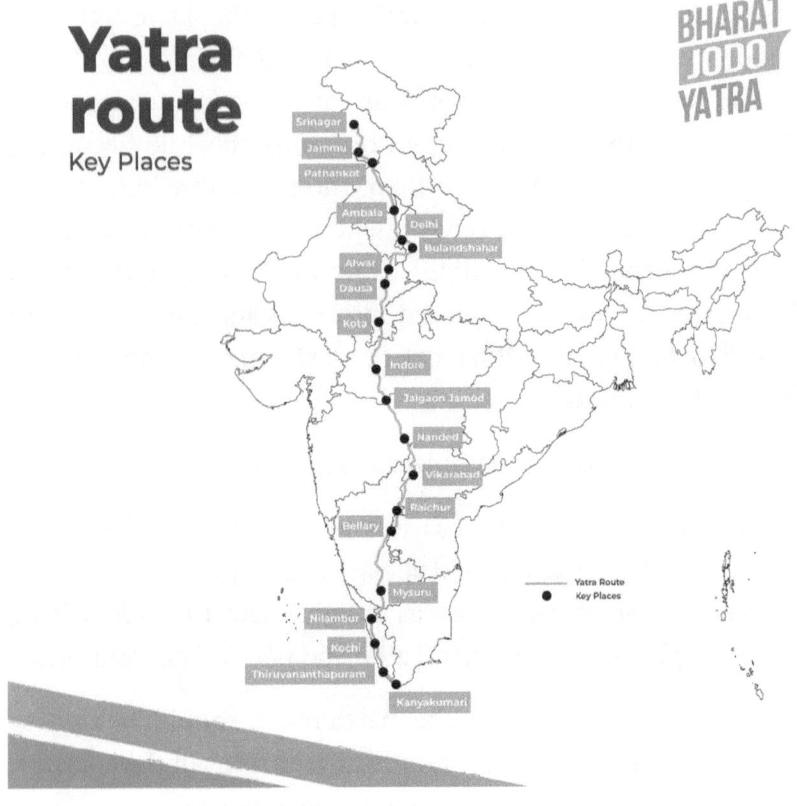

SOURCE: https://twitter.com/IYC

In the beginning, the Congress and even Rahul Gandhi never have thought of the bonanza success of the event. Even Rahul Gandhi, frankly accepted that he didn't hope for such a grand reception of the people, which the 'Bharat Jodo Yatra' able to garner the support. We shall see about the fate of the campaign in light of Congress's growth. Will "Bharat Jodo" imbue the Congress, or will it be just a "Tughlaqi" decision? They would tell you more about it. Anyway, the Yatra definitely, mean a lot for the Congress as well as RaGa to prove himself, unfortunately he hadn't been able to establish so far in the Indian political arena as a responsible and mature leader because some of his silly mistakes and secondly, probably because of the hypocritic Media.

The History of Yatras – In Indian politics, there is no shortage of journeys, some of which are truly epical. Indeed, Yatras is an integral part of the Indian political landscape ever since Gandhi's Dandi March in 1930. Its philosophy is deeply rooted in the social values of this diverse country. Since then, there had been several Padayatras, Rath Yatras etc., and these events, in fact, played pivotal role in transforming the fate of many politicians.

Right now, when Bharat Jodo Yatra, led by Rahul Gandhi is on the flare, we need to return into the past and take a joy of some extraordinary Yatras that really was payoff for the parties as well as leaders in respective states and whole country. Let's have the glimpses of such major events-

1   1991, the 'Rath Yatra' was instrumental in the BJP's emergence as a strong political force in the country. It was former president Murli Manohar Joshi, who 'Ekta Yatra' possibly supplemented Advani's 'Rath Yatra' in BJP's subsequent electoral triumphs. Though, this Rath Yatra also remained disputed because of bringing down the Babri Masjid.

2   At the state level, N. T. Rama Rao who pioneered the show business of Indian politics to revive this indigenous yatra culture as an effective political instrument in Independent India through his masterstroke of 'Chaitanya Rathnam'

    rally in 1982 which helped him to sweep the 1983 assembly elections in Andhra Pradesh.

3   Another one was the 'Praja Sankalpa Yatra' led by Y. S. Jagan Mohan Reddy covering more than 3500 Km by foot in 341 days prior to his party's sweeping success of his party in 2019 assembly elections in Andhra Pradesh.

4   In 2022, Uttar Pradesh assembly elections various political parties emerged through yatras. BJP launched 'Jan Ashirwad Yatra', Samajwadi Party went with Cycle calling it to be 'Cycle Yatra' and 'Kisan Nau Jawan Yatra', and Congress went among the voters through 'Pragati Yatra', and Dalit Swabhiman Yatra.

5   Then, there had been political yatras which are set for a long-term dividend. Chandra Shekhar's padayatra in 1983 from Kanyakumari to Delhi. In fact, this yatra would have yielded Chandra Shekhar, but Indira Gandhi's assassination diluted the impact of the padayatra in the 1984 Lok Sabha elections, but propelled him to the prime minister's 'Kursi' in 1990.

6   Another important Yatra was the 'Bharat Uday Yatra' which ahead of the 2004 general elections to highlight the achievements of Mr. Atal Behari Vajpayee's tenure of 6-years, but failed to infuse the spirit of 1990s.

The experiences of yatra do tell us that the success depends upon the offering and the electorates are ready to accept that. But if the party or the leader fails to either offer according to the wishes of the electorates or couldn't read the mind of the electorates then that can even lead toward the disaster or failure. In the light of such arguments, let's try to dissect the 'Bharat Jodo Yatra' led by RaGa that how much potential does it has? And will it be able to challenge the Modi regime?

Though, it is something which hidden in the womb of the future, but certainly there are some footprints that needs a discussion.

RaGa on the Ideological Front: It is no longer a secret that Congress has failed in navigating the divisive politics of the Hindu Right wing, and this has had been the worst impact on the party as a whole. Rahul Gandhi is the only leader who has emerged for the cause, despite widespread criticism for his reluctance to accept responsibility. But he continued to be the RSS's and BJP's strongest ideological foe, and this he demonstrated numerous times. Indeed, Rahul Gandhi has raised important questions on democracy, constitutionalism, and pluralism of the BJP but failed to cut through the ice with the Hindu vote bank, which the BJP has so assiduously created and nurtured through the malignity of victimhood and resentment. When Rahul Gandhi emphasized the significance of Nehruvian socialism, many elderly Congressmen's ears might have heard the reverberating tune of it after many years. Rahul Gandhi's anti-corporate rhetoric is a clear indication that the party's economic strand is changing. Instead of advocating for three decades of economic liberalization combined with welfareism, the party now places a greater emphasis on policies that promote distributive justice and social security programs. However, none of these things can take place on their own or win over voters unless the Congress expands its influence across a sizable segment of society through its policies and programs.

In order for the Congress to take on the BJP, RaGa again took the initiative to make its ideological position more understandable and consistent. And for that, the party needed to come down to the voters. Rahul Gandhi pushed the campaign "Bharat Jodo Yatra", which by now has become quite familiar among the wider section of Indians as well as quite populace at international level. The campaign has undoubtedly given the Congressmen newfound vigour and enthusiasm, and it has also significantly contributed to the large crowd's appearance on the streets to support Rahul Gandhi or even just to observe and listen to him. However, it isn't right moment to comment on the success of the Bharat Jodo Yatra in converting the pulling crowd into votes for the Congress.

As when I started this chapter, the "Bharat Jodo Yatra" already had arrived in New Delhi, the Indian capital, after traveling through a number of states, including Kerala, Tamil Nadu, Karnataka, Andhra Pradesh, Telangana, Maharashtra, Madhya Pradesh, Haryana, etc. However, Rahul Gandhi's capacity to relate to voters and the cohesion of Congress leaders are both positive indicators for the campaign. Marching from south and entering to Delhi must have been good experience for the Congress; where he entered into states led by the party which coalition partner of the Congress as well as also experienced the mood in the states presently ruled by BJP. For now one thing that can be said that this yatra had been crowed puller for RaGa, and surely, he himself wouldn't have accepted such overwhelming support. Hundreds and thousands of people walked with him, heard him and showed their solidarity behind this yatra.

"Bharat Jodo": Will It Be a New Dawn for Congress? – After many years, the Congress is finally on the move, and the Bharat Jodo Yatra is unquestionably the first and most significant step in the direction of making the Congress a living party. It is perceived as an effort by the party and Rahul Gandhi to establish a connection with the grassroots. This march is led by Rahul Gandhi and covers twelve states and two union territories. For the first time, Rahul Gandhi looked to be leading from the front and from the first day. He pitched this yatra as an attempt to connect with civil society from the word go, and he definitely got some good response in its first leg. In fact, Rahul Gandhi was able to muster some support from the members of civil society, and because of such efforts, Yogender Yadav became the companion of Rahul Gandhi in this yatra. In short, this small but crucial support was the initial success that allowed Rahul to go ahead with the yatra.

Rahul said and continues to call the Yatra "an effort to unite all Indians and protect its diversity at a time when it is under pressure from the Hindutva ideology and the BJP." What the Congress and Rahul Gandhi gained is what matters most now that the yatra has arrived in Delhi. In a sentence or two, we can say that the response from the public so far has been positive and that the yatra has been encouraging from the standpoint of drawing crowds. Man-to-man connection remained the key element of this yatra, where Rahul Gandhi succeeded in connecting the people. The ambitious "Bharat Jodo Yatra" reminds of the Hollywood movie Forrest Gump, but interestingly, here Rahul Gandhi walks and runs to bring about changes in the political scenario of India. Rahul Gandhi, who is extremely fit, walks effortlessly for 23 kilometres every day, whether it's hot outside or it's pouring rain. It is impossible to imagine that the top leaders of the BJP would do anything other than attack Rahul Gandhi. But this time such "lame attacks" seem to be failing. In fact, the more Rahul is attacked, the more youth and women seem to be drawn towards him.

As a leader, Rahul Gandhi seems to be more composed and mature than at other times. While the BJP leaders continue to make hate speeches, Rahul Gandhi continues to sing songs of harmony and diversity throughout the yatra. In stark contrast to the fact that he appeared calm, at ease, and composed when speaking to the public and the media during the press conference, he is no longer afraid to hold press conferences or to answer challenging questions. Though these are still early days to reach any kind of conclusion, if the same momentum continues, the BJP will go red. The next stage is now a little difficult for Rahul and the Congress; in particular, the real test will start when the Bharat Jodo Yatra enters Uttar Pradesh, where the two main parties, the Samajwadi Party and Bahujan Samaj Party's supremo Akhilesh Yadav and Mayawati, have already made it clear that they won't support the Bharat Jodo Yatra. As a result, RaGa and the Congress will have to pass a litmus test since the Congress lacks a robust organizational structure and a large support base. It has been the party that has been outcast from power for the last four decades. Because it is well known that the Road to Delhi passes through Uttar Pradesh, it was crucial for the Congress and RaGa to mobilize support and rally the public behind the Bharat Jodo Yatra. Second, demonstrating Congress' presence in Uttar Pradesh will also help the party gain support in the Hindi Belt, and to some extent this have been seeing, going in favour of Congress.

Right now, what Congress wants – is a leader and program that could at least pull the crowd onto their platform. Indeed, by no means is there a need to draw the conclusion that the crowds drawn to the Bharat Jodo Yatra will translate into votes. For that, the party still has a long way to go, and most importantly, they will have to communicate their ideas and vision and solidify the organization and structure that can bring the Congress voters to the polling booth. But the it is true that they have been successful in their first step.

Whatever the case may be, certainly for the time being, it will be advantageous that Congress is operating in a constructive manner and that its constituents are in an upbeat mood. They see the yatra as a landmark or the door to power in the near future. Whatever the result of this event, one thing is certain: Rahul Gandhi is advancing into a more mature, passionate, and determined leader than ever before. While the Congress as a party is looking more aggressive and united than before, it is unlikely that this portends that the Congress will attempt to invade the BJP's fortified stronghold. Just for that, Congress still has a lot of work to do. But the Bharat Jodo Yatra has lifted the Congress from its dismal position, where it continued to be just a few months ago.

However, now that the Bharat Jodo Yatra has reached the capital of India, one can assume its popularity from the wave of crowds, which definitely show that there is still space in the country for an inclusive, right-based form of politics that the Congress represents and can tap into. But still, we have to wait and watch to see how far it will transfer to voters during elections. But nevertheless, one can assume that Bharat Jodo Yatra has become synonymous with a narrative of unity, equality, and diversity, which needed to be translated into an economic and political blueprint.

The Timeline of Bharat Jodo Yatra in brief-

This is the timeline of the Bharat Jodo Yatra which is also comprised of important feature that shaped in different states from where the yatra crossed. This would give an idea how and what kind of people interacted with this yatra, further also give a mood of the vast society.

States	Time Period	Main Features
Tamil Nadu	Sep. 7-Sep. 10, 2022	Launching of the Yatra by Rahul Gandhi after paying tributes to his late father Rajiv Gandhi, Swami Vivekanand and the Tamil poet Thriuvalluvar. Several senior leaders like P. Chidambaram, Bhupesh Baghel etc. joined the yatra. Interacted sanitary workers and unemployed youth.
Kerala	Sep. 11-Sep. 29, 2022	Tenth evening, RaGa entered into Kerala with thousands of his supporters. The Kerala witnessed large turnout of the audience from wherever, the Bharat Jodo Yatra crossed. Though, several times the BJP local leadership tried to falsely alleged that the yatra was in solidarity with the PFI but it was in vain. The Yatra received a good response from all the section, while Hollywood actor John Cusack expressed his solidarity for this yatra and Rahul Gandhi.

States	Time Period	Main Features
Karnataka	Sep. 30-Oct. 15, 2022	The first BJP-ruled state where the Yatra entered. The atmosphere was unprecedented with huge crowd gathering with yatra. RaGa attacked on the BJP-RSS in his speech for spreading hate and violence in the state, further urge the people to spread love and peace for the which this yatra is all about. Mrs. Sonia Gandhi also joined the yatra. Among the prominent people who joined the yatra were the family of late journalist Gauri Lankesh, Congress leaders and even many social activists also joined.
Andhra Pradesh	Oct. 14-Oct. 19, 2022	In Andhra Pradesh while addressing press conference, RaGa attacked on the existing ruling party, and others for being the corrupt government in the state. Further, he promised special category status for Andhra if the Congress regain power at center.
Telangana	Oct. 27 – Nov. 02, 2022	The second phase of the yatra began after a break of three days from Telangana. Various section of people joined in the yatra – Tollywood actress Poonam Kaur, and Bollywood actress Pooja Bhatt, mother of late Dalit scholar Rohith Vemula, and many other also took part in this yatra while it was in Telangana.

States	Time Period	Main Features
Maharashtra	Nov. 07-Nov. 20, 2022	The actor and actress such as Sushant Singh, Amol Palekar, Riya Sen, Mona Ambe Gaonkar, Rashmi Desai, Akansha Puri, and Nagma joined the Bharat Jodo Yatra in Maharashtra. Social activist Medha Patkar, Mahatma Gandhi's grandson, Tushar Gandhi and several other also participated in the yatra. In one of the speech, RaGa took the ideological line in criticizing V. D. Savarkar for helping the British during the time of Indian National Movement.
Madhya Pradesh	Nov. 23-Nov. 27,2022	Another BJP ruled state where cunningly power was grabbed, despite Congress won the majority. The yatra was overwhelmingly received by the people of all section. Bharat Jodo Concert was held in Indore. Rapper Divine with MC Altaf and DJ Proof performed at the event.
Rajasthan	Dec.04-Dec.20, 2022	A first Congress ruled state where the yatra entered. Gehlot and Sachin Pilot accompanied in the yatra. Enthusiasm was seen in the Congress workers, as this is one of the states out of five where election is scheduled this year (2023). Former RBI Governor Raghu Rajan also accompanied to Rahul Gandhi in this yatra.

States	Time Period	Main Features
Haryana	Dec.21-Dec.23, 2022	DMK MP Kanimozhi joined the yatra in Haryana.
Delhi	Dec. 24, 2022	While entering Delhi, and reaching Red Fort after completing the second phase and 2800 Kms. RaGa addressing to audience said that ha had not seen any hatred or violence among while walking a long distance from Kanyakumari to Delhi.
Uttar Pradesh	Jan.02-Jan.05, 2023	After a short vacation of a week, the Yatra started for the third phase, and this time it entered into the most populated state of India, Uttar Pradesh. Most of the party of Uttar Pradesh wished Rahul Gandhi accept the BJP. Though, the yatra covered just three districts of Western UP. An unexpected enthusiasm was seen among the masses. In fact, RLD extended its whole-heartly support to the Yatra. Several places, RLD cadres and supporters joined the yatra. Former RAW chief A. S. Dulat, National President of Jammu & Kashmir Conference Farooq Abdullah, Bollywood actress Ritu Shivpuri was among several who participated in the yatra in Uttar Pradesh.

States	Time Period	Main Features
Punjab	Jan.10-Jan.17, 2023	RaGa visited the Golden Temple in Amritsar before commencing the yatra in the state. The yatra was received overwhelmingly by the people of the state. Late Sidhu Moose Wala's father and historian Mridula Mukherjee also participated in the event. Unfortunately, Congress lost one its Member of Parliament and a soldier of the party, Santokh Sing Chaudhary who died because of cardiac attack. As a mark of condolence, the yatra was cancelled for a day.
Himachal Pradesh	Jan. 18, 2023	The yatra remained in the state for just twenty-four Kms, and then entered into Jammu & Kashmir.
Jammu & Kashmir	Jan.19-Jan.29, 2023	The last state of the yatra, and all eyes were on the response that Rahul Gandhi will get over here. The atmosphere was in favor of the RaGa and the Congress, and it seems to be a good a news for the congress, as this state is also lined up for assembly election in the coming future. In the chilling cold, hundreds of people walked along with RaGa, women participation thrilled several eyecatchers. RaGa and Congress received support of all corners and all sections of people, including the Kashmiri Pandits.

States	Time Period	Main Features
		They shared their pain and anguish against the present central government, as they find isolated and cheated. Unfurling the national tricolor at Lal Chowk in Srinagar was the historic moment for all Indians. Several eminent people from various background walked with RaGa. Among them some prominent are actor-politician Urmila Matondkar, author Perumal Murugan, Param Veer Chakra recipient Captain Bana Singh and several leaders of various parties.

The yatra that started from Kanyakumari finally culminated in Jammu & Kashmir. This Yatra, I think was the longest march on foot by any Indian politician in the history of India, as claimed by the Congress. Though, it is too early to say about the profit and loss of the yatra in context of the Congress party and Rahul Gandhi. But certainly, the tempo of the congress seems to be on the upper end. And why not be so? Obviously, after a long time, the Congress party dare to go on the roads of India and in fact, also raised the issues against the BJP government. interestingly, they are prized with appraisal from the audience. Huge crowd of flocking had been observed in this yatra, and that is major boost for the Congress. Rahul Gandhi all through the showed sense of maturity and wisdom while addressing to media or public. This yatra has surfaced the ideological debate of whose India? Gandhi or Godse.

What is Next? – There isn't a doubt that the two events that took place in quick succession certainly brought new life to the Congress. Presently, Congress is being debated at the tea stall among the elderly, students, and youth. In a nutshell, it is attracting the crowd. And why not? Surely, the Bharat Jodo Yatra and the Congress presidential election have energized the entire party. The Congress party is now gaining ample space in newspapers and magazines, though TV media is still reluctant to show much about it, but social media has filled the space in a larger context.

The second element is the unexpectedly warm welcome that Rahul Gandhi has received in several states where his yatra passed by. Even Karnataka, the bastion as well as the laboratory of the BJP, foresees massive support for Rahul Gandhi and his Yatra. However, to understand the warmth of his welcome, it is important to look beyond the short, grudging news that television channels and mainline newspapers are serving. Indeed, I understand. One needs to peep inside the yatra, where he is amidst people of every age, religion, caste, and gender. He is found interacting with them, listening to their problems; in short, the people are seeing a kind of bonding with Rahul. It is a very different image of Rahul and his party that gives an impression of sincerity and innate decency. This change of perception is also apparent in the briefing reports of the hard-bitten reporters who are covering the Bharat Jodo Yatra.

For now, in particular, one can say that the Bharat Jodo Yatra effectively acted as a "Sanjeevni Booti" for the Congress, which eventually offered some hope in the dying Congress. This yatra has stolen the show in the political arena for some time. It is regularly talked about, discussed, and has become a matter of debate in political circles.

The BJP's political corridors, which frequently targeted the Congress for dynastic succession, were stunned by the announcement of a non-Gandhi Congress president. But the events have attracted the attention of different demographics that live in India. This gives it better chances if it continues to attack the BJP's policies and, at the same time, consolidates its organizational structure. Likewise, adopt its system of public governance.

Finally, the two events links to one another, as now it is a time when Congress can think of new experiments, and presently, they have started with, removing Rahul Gandhi from the burden of responsibility to handle the organizational issues of the party. As a result, he becomes more like a free bird who can concentrate on using his charm to spread the Congress' ideology, which he did successfully during the most recent Bharat Jodo Yatra. As a result, even though the Congress sought to distance itself from the Gandhi family, they continue to command the most respect and attention. For a very large section of Congress supporters, Congress is identical to the Gandhi family, and why not be so? They consistently stood up for the Congress ideology and supported the party wholeheartedly whenever Congress was in bad shape.

Can Congress make a comeback? Definitely, this question cannot be answered in 'Yes or No'. I would say it is just a beginning for the Congress. However, the Congress and Rahul Gandhi has able to attract the a section of the society, but still they require to do more, so that the party strengthen its foot among the people. The way large crowd of people was seen in the yatra, certainly, it is a positive sign for the Indian democracy and Congress. But then, the Congress has daunting task of strengthening the party structure at root level which is somewhat has weakened, and this they have to do within short span of time, if they want to give any sought of challenge to BJP in the upcoming general elections. Historically, the yatra would be remembered for long time for Rahul's hilarious effort, and the way he interact to the vast masses throughout the yatra, indeed it was amazing.

The bottom of the line is – Now, when the yatra has come to its end with a positive note. To a large extent, this yatra seems to be reaching near its objective. On the one hand, this yatra has established Rahul Gandhi as a strong-willed, indomitable, courageous and public-spirited leader, while on the other hand, resounding victory in the Himachal Pradesh Assembly Elections 2022, Karnataka and Telangana Assembly Elections 2023 and getting greater number of votes than BJP in Rajasthan, Madhya Pradesh and Chhattisgarh is underlining the political significance of this yatra also. It becomes duty for the all the leaders – of whatever rank and file they belong to, to be unitedly restructure the Congress organization and further take the party's ideology among the wider section of both; rural and urban people. The success of the yatra needs to harvested, and that alone cannot be done by few leaders, but the Congress as unified party needs work tirelessly to regain the lost legacy.

Appendix and Reference

1. (Indian National Congress and the Role in Indian Independence: A Brief History)

1   R. Randeep. India's secret history: 'A holocaust, one where millions disappeared...' dated – August 24, 2007. Published in – The Guardian. Link – https://www.theguardian.com/world/2007/aug/24/india.randeepramesh

2   History of the Indian National Congress. Link – https://en.m.wikipedia.org/wiki/History_of_the_Indian_National_Congress

3   "March to socialism under Prime Minister Indira Gandhi". *The Economic Times*. The Times Group. Bennett, Coleman & Co. Ltd. 24 August 2011.

4   The moderates, led by Gopal Krishna Gokhale, Pherozeshah Mehta, and Dadabhai Naoroji, held firm to calls for negotiations and political dialogue. Gokhale criticized Tilak for encouraging acts of violence and disorder. The Congress of 1906 did not have public membership, and thus Tilak and his supporters were forced to leave the party.

5   Shakeel Anwar. Dated – July 30, 2018. List of political organization before the establishment of Congress. Link – https://www.jagranjosh.com/general-knowledge/list-of-political-organizations-before-the-establishment-of-congress-1532946932-1

6   British Raj. Link – https://en.m.wikipedia.org/wiki/British_Raj

7   N. Niaz Ahmed. Dated – 1986-87. History of Indian Congress, 1885-1950, A selected Annotated Bibliography.

8   A timeline of Congress history. Link-https://www.india-seminar.com/2003/526/526%20timeline.htm

9   Bipin Chandra. (2008). India Since Independence. Published by – Penguin

2. (Congress and Its Ideology)

1   N. Niaz Ahmed. Dated – 1986-87. History of Indian Congress, 1885-1950, A selected Annotated Bibliography.

2   Moderates, Extremists and Revolutionaries. NCERT.

3   Bipin Chandra. (2008). India Since Independence. Published by – Penguin

4   Shikha Goyal. (2022). Independence Day 2022: Summary of Indian National Movement. Published – Jagran Josh. Link – https://www.jagranjosh.com/general-knowledge/summary-of-indian-national-movement-1465033301-1

5   The Moderate and Extremist Phase of Congress. Link – https://unacademy.com/content/railway-exam/study-material/modern-history-of-india/the-moderate-and-extremist-phase-of-congress/

6   A timeline of Congress history. Link-https://www.india-seminar.com/2003/526/526%20timeline.htm

3. (Role of Congress in Building the Nation (1950-1975))

1   Brief history of Congress – 1945-1955. Indian National Congress. Link – https://www.inc.in/brief-history-of-congress/1945-1955

2   Bipin Chandra. (2008). India Since Independence. Published by – Penguin

3 The parties that contested India's first General Election. Publisher – The Wire.

4 J. S, Grewal. (2018). The Akali-Congress confrontation: (1952-1955). Published by – Oxford Academic. Link – https://doi.org/10.1093/oso/9780199467099.003.0020

5 apoorav@mappingdigiworld.com. Jawaharlal Nehru and the Indian National Congress. Published by – Map of India.link–https://www.mapsofindia.com/personalities/ nehru/nehru-and-indian-national-congress.html

6 Bidyut Chakrabarty. Jawaharlal Nehru and Planning, 1938-41: India at the Crossroad. Modern Asian Studies 26, 2 (1992), pp. 275-287. Printed in – Cambridge University Press, Great Britain. Link – https://www.jstor.org/stable/ 312676

7 Suranjan Das. (2001). The Nehru years in Indian Politics. Edinburgh paper in South Asian Studies. Link – WP16_ Suranjan_Das.pdf

8 John Callaghan. (2007). Jawaharlal Nehru and the communist party. Published by – Taylor & Francis Online. Link – https://www.tandfonline.com/doi/abs/10.1080/ 13523279108415096?journalCode=fjcs19

4. (An Era of Success and Downfall: 1975 to 2000)

1 Neeti Nair. (2020). Mindless devotion to Congress politics is no substitute for a thoughtful reckoning of the past. Published by – Indian Express Daily Newspaper. Link – https://indianexpress.com/article/opinion/columns/ congress-leadership-rahul-gandhi-cwc-history- 6574083/

2 Bipin Chandra. (2008). India Since Independence. Published by – Penguin

3   Ajay Kumar & Prabhu Chawla. (2014). Indian National Congress passes through a crisis of self-confidence. Published – India Today. Link – https://www.indiatoday.in/magazine/special-report/story/19860115-indian-national-congress-passes-through-a-crisis-of-self-confidence-800477-1986-01-14

4   Martand Jha. (2017). How the Indian National Congress lost India. publisher – The Diplomat. Link – https://thediplomat.com/2017/04/how-the-indian-national-congress-lost-india/

5   Sarim Naved. (2022). What's Really wrong with the Congress. Publisher – The Wire. Link – https://thewire.in/politics/whats-really-wrong-with-the-congress

6   Milan Vaishnav & Danielle Smogard. (2014). A New era in Indian Politics. published in – Carnegie Endowment for International Peace. Link – https://carnegieendowment.org/2014/06/10/new-era-in-indian-politics-pub-55883

5. (Inclusion of Capitalism and Syncretism: A New Style of Congress)

1   Jayant Sinha. (2017). New economy for new India: Fundamental changes put in place for an open, changes put in place for an open, transparent, competitive and innovation-driven economy. Publisher – The Times of India. Link – https://timesofindia.indiatimes.com/blogs/toi-edit-page/new-economy-for-new-india-fundamental-changes-put-in-place-for-an-open-transparent-competitive-and-innovation-driven-economy/

2   Bipin Chandra. (2008). India Since Independence. Published by – Penguin

3   Politics and economy. Link – https://www.britannica.com/place/India/Politics-and-the-economy

4   Milan Vaishnav & Danielle Smogard. (2014). A New era in Indian Politics. published in – Carnegie Endowment for International Peace. Link – https://carnegieendowment.org/2014/06/10/new-era-in-indian-politics-pub-55883

5   Shekhar Gupta. (2021). Economic ideology is the new binary in Indian politics as Modi swerves Right & Rahul Left. Publish in – The Print. Link – https://theprint.in/national-interest/the-new-battle-lines-in-indian-politics-modis-private-sector-push-vs-rahuls-socialism/604373/

6. (Congress: A Party of Idea and Changes*)*

1   Bipin Chandra. (2008). India Since Independence. Published by – Penguin

2   John R. Bond. (2017). Ideological change in Congress? Occasionally, but not quickly and not everywhere. Published in Research Gate (conference paper). Link – https://www.researchgate.net/publication/313282906_Ideological_Change_in_Congress_Occasionally_but_Not_Quickly_and_Not_Everywhere

3   Bidyut Chakrabarty. (2008). Indian Politics and Society since Independence. Published by – Routledge Taylor & Francis. ISBN 0-203-92767-2

4   Md. Ayub Mallick. (2013). Ideology of the Indian National Congress: Political economy of socialism and socialistic pattern of society. IOSR Journal Of Humanities And Social Science (IOSR-JHSS). Volume 12, Issue 2 (May. – Jun. 2013), PP 96-112. e-ISSN: 2279-0837, p-ISSN: 2279-0845. www.Iosrjournals.Org

7. (Crisis of Leadership in Congress)

1 Anuja, "Two years since leadership crisis, Congress's bigger trouble continues to be from State Units", *The Wire*, 2 July 2021, https://thewire.in/politics/congress-leadership-crisis-state-units-disarray-elections.

2 ANI. (2022). Congress leadership crisis: G-23 leaders to meet Gandhis soon. Publishe by – The Indian Express. Link – https://www.newindianexpress.com/nation/2022/mar/18/congress-leadership-crisis-g-23-leaders-to-meet-gandhis-soon-say-sources-2431522.html

3 Bipin Chandra. (2008). India Since Independence. Published by – Penguin

4 Priya Sahgal. (2022). Congress leadership crisis. published by – The Daily Guardian. Link – https://thedailyguardian.com/congress-leadership-crisis/

5 Vinod Rai. (2021). Congress leadership crisis: What it portends for the party? Published by – ISAS Insight. Link – https://www.isas.nus.edu.sg/papers/congress-leadership-crisis-what-it-portends-for-the-party/

6 Ajay Ashirwad Mahaprashasta. (2022). Central leadership gets a bad rap, but the roots of Congress's problem lie in state. Published by – The Wire. Link – https://thewire.in/politics/congress-gandhis-state-leadership

7 (2020). Leadership issues troubled Congress in 2020, caused their electoral fortunes further decline.

8 Martand Jha. (2017). How the Indian National Congress lost India. published in – The Diplomat. Link – https://thediplomat.com/2017/04/how-the-indian-national-congress-lost-india/

9 Swami Naved. (2022). What really wrong with the Congress. Published by – The Wire. Link – https://thewire.in/politics/whats-really-wrong-with-the-congress

10 Neeti Nair. (2020). Mindless devotion to Congressi politics is no substitute for a thoughtful reckoning of the past. Published in – The Indian Express. Link – https://indianexpress.com/article/opinion/columns/congress-leadership-rahul-gandhi-cwc-history-6574083/

8. (A Beginning of New Politics in the Times of New Economy)

1 Milan Vaishnav & Danielle Smogard. (2014). A New era in Indian Politics. published in – Carnegie Endowment for International Peace. Link – https://carnegieendowment.org/2014/06/10/new-era-in-indian-politics-pub-55883

2 Jeffry Frieden. (20220). The political economy of economic policy. International Monetary Fund. Link-https://www.imf.org/en/Publications/fandd/issues/2020/06/political-economy-of-economic-policy-jeff-frieden

3 Bipin Chandra. (2008). India Since Independence. Published by – Penguin

4 Barun Mitra. (2021). Political of economic reforms: Real lessons from 1991. Published by – Friedrich Naumann Foundation. Link – https://theprint.in/campus-voice/congress-didnt-do-much-to-tackle-accusations-thrown-at-party-and-these-stayed/551344/

5 Jos Mooji. (2012). The politics of economic reforms in India: A Review of the Literature. Published by – Cambridge University Press. Link – https://www.cambridge.org/core/books/abs/rethinking-indian-political-institutions/politics-of-economic-reforms-in-india-a-review-of-the-literature/521876179C0104CCA727584B21F3B730

6 Jayant Sinha. (2017). New economy for new India: Fundamental changes put in place for an open, transparent,

competitive and innovation-driven economy. Published by – The Times of India. link – https://timesofindia. indiatimes.com/blogs/toi-edit-page/new-economy-for-new-india-fundamental-changes-put-in-place-for-an-open-transparent-competitive-and-innovation-driven-economy/

7 Shekar Gupta. (2021). Economic ideology is the new binary in Indian politics as Modi swerves Right & Rahul Left. Published in – The Print. Link – https://theprint.in/national-interest/the-new-battle-lines-in-indian-politics-modis-private-sector-push-vs-rahuls-socialism/604373/

8 Jeffry Frieden. (2020). The political economy of economic policy. Published Report – International Monetary Fund. Link – https://www.imf.org/en/Publications/fandd/issues/2020/06/political-economy-of-economic-policy-jeff-frieden

9. (Organizational and Structural Crisis Within Congress: Tearing the Hope Apart)

1 Congress' organizational structure weakened due to vacancies in departments, cells: Sources. Published – February 24, 2020. The New Indian Express. Link – https://www.newindianexpress.com/nation/2020/feb/24/congress-organisational-structure-weakened-due-to-vacancies-in-departments-cells-sources-2107497.html

2 Ajay Gudavarthy. (2022). The Congress has a structural crisis, not just loss of connect. Published by – News Click. Link – https://www.newsclick.in/congress-has-structural-crisis-not-just-loss-connect

3   Sudha Ramachandran. (2015). Indian National Congress: A Party in crisis. published in – The Diplomat. Link – https://thediplomat.com/2015/10/indian-national-congress-a-party-in-crisis/

4   Sanjay Kapoor. (2020). The Indian National Congress' identity crisis. link – http://emocracy/the-indian-national-congress-identity-crisis-4694/

10. (The Cocktail of old Strategy and New Politics)

1   Milan Vaishnav & Danielle Smogard. (2014). A New era in Indian Politics. published in – Carnegie Endowment for International Peace. Link – https://carnegieendowment.org/2014/06/10/new-era-in-indian-politics-pub-55883

2   Suhas Palshikar. (2017). India's Second dominant party. Published by – Economic & Political weekly. Vol. 52, Issue No. 11. Link – https://www.epw.in/journal/2017/11/web-exclusives/indias-second-dominant-party-system.html

3   Murli Krishnan. (2022). Can India's grand old party regain its former glory. Published by – DW. Link – https://www.dw.com/en/can-indias-grand-old-party-regain-its-former-glory/a-63414281

4   Zoya Hasan. (2022). A grand old party, the demanding paths to its revival. Published by – The Hindu.com, link – https://www.thehindu.com/opinion/lead/a-grand-old-party-the-demanding-path-to-its-revival/article65376382.ece

5   Shikha Mukerjee. (2021). As Indian polity mature, new politics is on the risw. Published by – Deccan Chronicle. Link – https://www.deccanchronicle.com/opinion/

columnists/051221/shikha-mukerjee-as-indian-polity-matures-new-politics-is-on-the-ris.html

6   Andrew Marantz. (2021). Are we entering a new political era? Published in – The New Yorker. Link – https://www.newyorker.com/magazine/2021/05/31/are-we-entering-a-new-political-era

7   A. K. Bhattacharya. (2021). Fragile politics: A necessary and sufficient condition for reform. Published in – Observer Research Foundation. Link – https://www.orfonline.org/expert-speak/fragile-politics-necessary-sufficient-condition-reforms/

8   Sandeep Phukan. (2022). Do ypung leaders have a future in the Congress? Published in – The Hindu.com. link – https://www.thehindu.com/news/national/do-young-leaders-have-a-future-in-the-congress/article65264892.ece

11. (Narrative of Upliftment)

1   Sarim Naved. (2022). What's really wrong with the Congress. Published in – The Wire. Link – https://www.thehindu.com/news/national/do-young-leaders-have-a-future-in-the-congress/article65264892.ece

2   Satish Mishra. (2019). End of Congress or a new beginning. Published in – Observer Research Foundation. Link – https://www.orfonline.org/expert-speak/end-of-congress-or-a-new-beginning-52845/

3   Team Frontline. (2022). Rise and fall of the Congress. Published in – Frontline. Link – https://frontline.thehindu.com/politics/rise-and-fall-of-the-congress-maharashtra-uttar-pradesh-south-india-goa/article66069947.ece

4   Congress Sandesh. (2016). Commitment for upliftment of poor, unprivileged, downtrodden is in the DNA of the Congress. Link – https://inc.in/congress-sandesh/development/commitment-for-upliftment-of-poor-unprivileged-downtrodden-is-in-the-dna-of-the-congress

12. (Will Mallikarjun Kharge's Presidential Term Be Reinventor for Congress?)

1   A timeline of Congress history. Link-https://www.india-seminar.com/2003/526/526%20timeline.htm

2   Amrit Dhillon. (2022). India's Congress party appoints first non-Gandhi president in 24 years. Published in – The guardian. Link – https://www.theguardian.com/world/2022/oct/19/india-congress-party-appoints-first-non-gandhi-president-in-24-years

3   Murli Krishnan. (2022). Can a non-Gandhi president revive India's Congress party. Published in – DW.com. link – https://www.dw.com/en/india-can-the-new-congress-president-revive-the-party/a-63504288

4   Press Trust of India. (2023). Mallikarjun Kharge becomes first non-Gandhi Congress president in 24 years. Published in – Business Standard. Link – https://wap.business-standard.com/article/politics/mallikarjun-kharge-becomes-first-non-gandhi-congress-president-in-24-years-122101900593_1.html

5   Outlook Web Desk. (2022). Congress Presidential polls: non-Congress who became party chiefs before Sonia Gandhi. Published in – Outlook Web Desk. Link – https://www.outlookindia.com/national/congress-presidential-polls-non-gandhis-who-became-parties-chiefs-before-sonia-gandhi-news-230393

6   Sandeep Phukan. (2022). Challenges aplenty for Congress president-elect Mallikarjun Kharge. Published – The Hindu. Link – https://www.thehindu.com/news/national/key-challenges-that-mallikarjun-kharge-faces-as-congress-president/article66032727.ece

13. (Bharat Jodo Yatra and Impact on Congress)

1   Timeline of Bharat Jodo Yatra. Link – https://en.m.wikipedia.org/wiki/Timeline_of_Bharat_Jodo_Yatra

2   Wikipedia. Bharat Jodo Yatra. Link – https://en.m.wikipedia.org/wiki/Bharat_Jodo_Yatra

3   Outlook Web Desk. (2022). Bharat Jodo Yatra: Here is a look at some other key 'Yatras' by Indian Politicians. Published in – Outlook. Link – https://www.outlookindia.com/national/with-start-of-congress-bharat-jodo-yatra-here-is-a-look-at-some-key-yatras-undertaken-by-politicians-in-india-news-221953

4   Saubhadra Chatterji. (2016). How Yatras have turned the tide for Indian politicians at different times. Published in – The Hindustan Times. Link – https://www.hindustantimes.com/india-news/how-yatras-have-turned-the-tide-for-indian-politicians-at-different-times/story-elIoIQqLMO3Z3XoNvCd6OO_amp.html#aoh=16724094282337&referrer=https%3A%2F%2Fwww.google.com&_tf=From%20%251%24s

5   Vidhatri Rao. (2022). Yatra politics pver the years: From Advani's 'Rath Yatra' to Congress's 'Bharat Jodo Yatra'. Published in – The Indian Express. Link – https://indianexpress.com/article/political-pulse/yatra-politics-over-the-years-from-advanis-rath-yatra-to-congresss-bharat-jodo-yatra-8032540/

6   Atanu Biswas. (2022). Many shades of 'Yatras'. Published in – Deccan Herald. Link – https://www.deccanherald.com/opinion/panorama/many-shades-of-yatras-1154485.html

7   Timesofindia.com. (2022). Congress's Bharat Jodo Yatra: Politics, logistics and evolution of 'padyatras'. Published in – The Times of India. Link – https://m.timesofindia.com/india/congs-bharat-jodo-yatra-politics-logistics-evolution-of-padyatras/amp_articleshow/94098527.cms

Special thanks to https://translate.google.co.in/because without its help it would have been very difficult for a Hindi speaking writer like me to write books.

www.ingramcontent.com/pod-product-compliance
Lightning Source LLC
Chambersburg PA
CBHW031535150726
47990CB00001B/182